V. P. Horbulin, O. F. Byelov,
O. V. Lytvynenko

Ukraine's National Security

Geneva Centre for the
Democratic Control of Armed Forces
(DCAF)

LIT

V. P. Horbulin, O. F. Byelov, O. V. Lytvynenko

Ukraine's National Security

An Agenda for the Security Sector

LIT

∞

Gedruckt auf alterungsbeständigem Werkdruckpapier entsprechend
ANSI Z3948 DIN ISO 9706

Bibliographic information published by the Deutsche Nationalbibliothek
The Deutsche Nationalbibliothek lists this publication in the Deutsche Nationalbibliografie; detailed bibliographic data are available in the Internet at http://dnb.d-nb.de.

ISBN 978-3-643-80045-9

A catalogue record for this book is available from the British Library

Dufourstr. 31
CH-8008 Zürich
Tel. +41 (0) 44-251 75 05
Fax +41 (0) 44-251 75 06
e-Mail: zuerich@lit-verlag.ch
http://www.lit-verlag.ch

LIT VERLAG Dr. W. Hopf
Berlin 2010
Fresnostr. 2
D-48159 Münster
Tel. +49 (0) 2 51-620 320
Fax +49 (0) 2 51-922 60 99
e-Mail: lit@lit-verlag.de
http://www.lit-verlag.de

Distribution:

In Germany: LIT Verlag Fresnostr. 2, D-48159 Münster
Tel. +49 (0) 2 51-620 32 22, Fax +49 (0) 2 51-922 60 99, e-Mail: vertrieb@lit-verlag.de

In Austria: Medienlogistik Pichler-ÖBZ, e-mail: mlo@medien-logistik.at

In Switzerland: B + M Buch- und Medienvertrieb, e-mail: order@buch-medien.ch

In the UK: Global Book Marketing, e-mail: mo@centralbooks.com

In North America by:

Transaction Publishers
New Brunswick (U.S.A.) and London (U.K.)

Transaction Publishers
Rutgers University
35 Berrue Circle
Piscataway, NJ 08854

Phone: +1 (732) 445 - 2280
Fax: + 1 (732) 445 - 3138
for orders (U. S. only):
toll free (888) 999 - 6778
e-mail: orders@transactionpub.com

CONTENTS

Preface

Western observers of Ukrainian Security Policy and its dialectics have, for a long time, been reduced to comments and analysis by Western experts and/or Ukrainians teaching at higher learning institutions in Europe and the US. Alternative Russian sources have retained a distinctive flavour of their own.

The present volume would seem to be the first collection of essays by Ukrainian senior experts in office. The contributions to this volume, first published in Ukrainian in 2008, are thus first-hand, of importance not only for their contents, but also for allowing the reader to judge for themselves the level of the security-political discourse in Ukraine. It is understood that the authors are giving their own views, which do not necessarily coincide with established views of the facilitating agency, the Geneva Centre for the Democratic Control of Armed Forces.

The Geneva Centre for the Democratic Control of Armed Forces (DCAF) has continuously cooperated with the Ukrainian parliament and defence ministry since its establishment in the year 2000. The present work of the Centre is focused on Ukraine's Strategic Defence Review and defence management reform in general in what has turned out to be a most inspiring and enriching cooperation programme for all those involved.

DCAF would like to thank O. Myshlovska and A. Arjun for their careful translation and language editing, and A. Marillet and S. Imobersteg for their diligent technical editing.

Geneva, March 8, 2010

Philipp Fluri, Ph.D.
Deputy Director DCAF

Foreword

Over the past years, the national security of Ukraine has been hotly debated among domestic and foreign politicians, experts and researchers. Numerous publications—some academic and others of a more propagandistic nature—have been written on the subject.

These publications, in the authors' opinion, however, have failed to provide a comprehensive picture of the phenomenon of national security to the Ukrainian society and political elite. There is a perception that *national security* is akin to a pendulum with how far it swings contingent on global events of pivotal importance or alternatives to events outside human control. Complex mechanisms of national security management, including crucial psychological factors such as awareness and human will (individual or collective), remain unaddressed.

For example, the active implementation of the Membership Action Plan (MAP) in the framework of Ukraine's potential NATO membership in 2008 became one of the more widely discussed subjects. Participants focused their attention mostly on external issues or propaganda. Intense discussions about the plan and in particular an increase in Ukraine's investments towards NATO membership have failed to yield any clear and direct benefits. Furthermore, any considerations of NATO issues within the wider context of community development have been almost nonexistent. Understanding the issue of national security and the reasons for Ukraine's entry into the NATO alliance would ultimately allow the dilemma between 'neutrality and participation in one of the collective security systems', to be resolved.

The question of Ukrainian-Russian relations has also been discussed more intensely. The military conflict in the Caucasus in August 2008 aggravated the situation, with both sides issuing trenchant declarations and offensive notes and forms. Articles on recognised Russian internet sites also discussed the scenarios of a Russian-Ukrainian war.[1]

These problems became even more acute both before and after the Russian-Georgian war, when the question of the use of military force to resolve international disputes emerged on the agenda in the post-Soviet space.

---

1 Dzhadan I. Operatsiya, 'Mekhanicheskiy apel'sin', http://www.russ.ru/stat-i/operaciya-mehanicheskij-apel-sin

Many politicians and experts consider the next location for the realisation of the 'Ossetian-Georgian scenario' will become Ukraine, above all the Crimea.

There is a real danger of the loss of control of information and Ukraine's transition to self-maintaining status, particularly when the subsequent acts of players are determined not consciously but rather by an inherent logic of the culture of confrontation.

All of this leads to an important change in the climate surrounding national security both internal and external to Ukraine. As a result, it would appear therefore to render current approaches to management in the field of national security obsolete.

The understanding of the present critical threats and trends determined the theme of this book. The book analyses the current security situation and the manner by which it may be improved. Euro-Atlantic integration is one of the critical themes of the book. Essentially, the necessity to devise a new agenda for the national security of Ukraine is the focus.

Not only Ukrainian but also leading European experts agree that this is a critical time. James Sherr (Head of the Russia and Eurasia Program at Chatham House) came to similar conclusions in his article, 'The Politics of National Destruction'[2] as did Aleksander Kwaśniewski, former president of Poland and other experts in the field.

This book analyses a number of current problems in the area of national security of Ukraine and provides neither exhaustive nor perfect formula for their resolution.

The purpose of writing is to encourage and stimulate debate about Ukraine's potential membership of NATO, not to present a pro-membership or prescriptive discourse.

It is widely accepted that Ukraine's development is characterised by two key processes. Firstly, that it is fundamentally a society in transition, gradually moving from the phenomena referred to in the West as communism or real socialism. This process involves a series of changes, in particular its economic and political relations (political and state regimes), the legal system, public institutions, the emergence of civil society and its separation from the state (the Soviet state did not recognise the existence of an independent civil society even in theory).

The second process is Ukraine's journey from post-imperial and post-colonial transition to its emergence as an independent state. This process has to be examined from a perspective which takes into account that both a state and a modern nation occur simultaneously. Each of these developments deserves a discussion and will be addressed in respective chapters of the book.

---

2 Sherr J., Polityka natsional'noho ruynuvannya, Dzerkalo tyzhnya, 02.08.2008.

The topics addressed are the constitutional framework required for the functioning of the security sector of Ukraine, the development of the system of strategic planning, management of the sector and reform of the security services.

The basis of the first and fifth chapters of this book were materials revised from the brochure by V.P. Horbulin and O.V. Lytvynenko 'National Security: the Ukrainian Dimension' (Kyiv: IPNB, 2008, 101 pages), as well as research on the development of the Ukrainian security sector.

The authors are mindful of the contradictions and even the provocative nature of the ideas presented in this book and the absence of traditional 'correctness' typical of Ukrainian research on this subject. However, we are adamant that discussions on the strategic problems of national security must—in as far as is possible—be candid because political correctness cannot justify the cost of errors made hitherto. The pace of the processes in Europe and the rest of the world are such that even the bluntest provocation can be followed just in a few months by news reports on conflicts and events that are blown out of proportion.

The authors are also conscious that some themes highlighted in this book are not addressed in a comprehensive way and require additional research. At the same time, they are aware of the amount of work that would have been needed and are convinced that additional work on these subjects would have postponed the publication of the book by several years.

On account of the feedback we received from our 'benevolent' critics in a previous edition of this book, we would like to stress that it is not the intention to provide any recommendations to politicians, experts or citizens. This book is an attempt to find ways to transform the substantive and vital pattern of our society's life, many aspects of which until now have unfortunately been determined by the spirit of suicidal 'ruin' (that is low self-esteem and stereotypes) and of Ukrainians being blamed for Ukraine's defeats by 'hostile neighbours near and far'.[3]

3 Dzyuba I. Pislyamova, in Oleh Ol'zhych. Dukh Ruyiny. Kyiv: Smoloskyp, 2008, p. 46.

Introduction

This is not the first time that a book about Ukraine has appeared at a significant turning point in its history. But it is the first such occasion since Ukraine's last president, Viktor Yushchenko, was inaugurated in January 2005. Moreover, this is a particularly significant book. All three authors occupied critical positions in Ukraine's security establishment not only during Yushchenko's presidency, but during that of his predecessor, Leonid Kuchma. Today of all times, their experience and insights matter, because what is most important at a dramatic moment is perspective. The reform of Ukraine's security services has been an imperative since their creation. Few outside the most expert circles are aware of this. It is vital that wider circles of people understand continuities as well as changes in Ukraine's development, the growth of professionalism as well as careerism, and the role of geopolitics as well as politics, especially at a time when the inauguration of Ukraine's new president, Viktor Yanukovych, leads many to fear that everything achieved will be lost. Most vital of all is to understand Ukraine, for only by doing this can we form a view, for better or for worse, about what is possible and what is not.

Each of the authors of this volume has been obliged to serve individuals, but all have been dedicated to serving their country. Since 1991, Volodymyr Horbulin's fortunes have ebbed and flowed with the fortunes of Ukraine's statehood. As Secretary of and inspiration behind Ukraine's National Security and Defence Council (NSDC), Horbulin gave energy and direction to three cardinal tasks: the establishment of an integrated system of national security and defence, the transformation of the roles and ethos of that system's military and civil components, and the engagement of international partners. That the first and most urgent of these tasks was accomplished without chaos and upheaval is a national and collective achievement, but it is also Horbulin's personal triumph. That the second and most problematic of these tasks attracted overall backing from President Kuchma during his first term (1994-99) and increasing obstruction during his second (1999-2004) was a source of distress to him, a matter of mounting concern to Ukraine's international partners and an anxiety for the country.

It is testimony to the scale of Ukraine's transformation that this publication's second author, Oleksandr Belov, is now at the forefront of public discussion as well as official policymaking in the sphere of security sector reform. Whatever post he held, for most of the period in question he has been *eminence grise* of the Chairman of the Security Services of Ukraine (SBU). This has not always been a congenial task. Not all chairmen have shared his commitment to the country's Euro-Atlantic course, let alone Western values. For much of the pre-Orange period, Belov's job was damage limitation. For much of the Orange period, he sought to curb enthusiasm on the part of Ukraine's partners and amateurism on the part of the SBU's new political masters.

The third author, Oleksandr Lytvynenko, is an exemplary and unusually forthright member of the new wave of thinkers and security service professionals in the country. By now, he is a seasoned practitioner after years as an 'insider's insider' in four institutions: the NSDC, SBU and National Institute of Strategic Studies (NISS)—and, latterly, the more recently established Institute of National Security Problems, which like the NISS is subordinate to the President of Ukraine. He is also one of the country's leading and most outspoken experts on the relationship between Ukraine's external and internal security problems. He has written (most frequently for *The Day* and *Zerkalo Nedeli* and often with Horbulin himself) with particular prescience and candour on the uglier aspects of Ukraine's democratisation, including the growth of nativist and extremist sentiment within communities disillusioned or alienated by changes inside the country.

For all of their differences, the authors of this volume share three abiding convictions. The first is that the armed forces and security services be staffed by well-motivated professionals, loyal to Ukraine and committed to advancing its interests as an independent and democratic state. If the state obliges them to serve a narrower and more capricious scheme of interests, these qualities will disappear. If it does not properly finance these services, they will be forced to become entrepreneurial with the skills at their disposal and lose society's respect as well as their own. If the services, for their part, do not understand the country's wider, non-security related scheme of priorities, let alone the needs of the national economy, they will demand too much of their country and damage it. The politicisation or privatisation of these services is as grave a threat to national security as the emergence of a Bonapartist spirit within them.

The second conviction is that armed forces and security services must be accountable to political authorities who, in turn, are answerable to the law and the electorate. But no matter how civilianised or democratic, civil-democratic control will suffer if the controllers, their advisers and the broader community of experts and opinion leaders fail to acquire a reasonable degree of literacy in matters of national security and defence. Armed forces must be well subordinated, but they also must be free to speak, and they must be confident that what they say will be understood. 'Shut up and obey' is as dangerous a principle in democracies as it is in dictatorships, and it is undemocratic in itself. In recognition of these realities, the authors have supported the strengthening of NGOs, the widening of public discussion and, through such bodies as the Public Council of the SBU, the involvement of qualified outsiders in the formation of defence and security policy.

The third conviction is that Ukraine cannot stand alone. Leonid Kuchma, who wrote a book entitled *Ukraine is Not Russia*, also stated that 'Ukraine is not Switzerland'. Not only has Ukraine not been blessed with the same 'geopolitical cornucopia' (in the words of another preeminent security professional, Yevhen Marchuk), its GDP per capita is one twentieth to one thirty-fifth that of Europe's neutral states, it is not a member of the EU, and it has only begun to develop the civic confidence and disciplines that these states take for granted. The authors are convinced that NATO membership would be 'instrumental in enabling Ukraine to depart from its post-imperial past', providing it with 'the means of strengthening its state institutions' and 'enabling its participation in the mechanisms and procedures' of a 'global world'. At the same time, they do not idealise NATO. 'It does not provide absolute guarantees but will give a certain freedom of action in the future and confidence through support'. But membership of the Russian-dominated Collective Security Treaty Organisation (CSTO) would do nothing of the kind.

It is a return to the place from which Ukraine departed seventeen years ago….Its response is based on very different values [to NATO's]. Becoming party to such a collective would involve taking on an additional load of Russian problems, which together with domestic ones would almost surely destroy Ukraine's independence.

The chapters that follow present the contours of Ukraine's national security system and say much about its evolution. They describe the country's geopolitical circumstances, the mechanisms of NATO-Ukraine cooperation, the sociology of Ukraine's political and security elite and the knowledge and information base of society. Finally, they offer a number of insights about the country's heritage, shortcomings and potential, as well as an analysis of the thinking and policy of its most significant and problematic neighbour, Russia. The balance of this introduction provides a synoptic complement and counterpoint to the exposition that follows.

Starting from Naught

Outside Ukraine, many still fail to appreciate how unfavourable its starting conditions were. Although the country inherited 1.4 million men under arms (not including police), fully 30 per cent of the military personnel of the former USSR in 1991, it did not inherit an army, let alone a Ministry of Defence or General Staff. It inherited powerful force groupings, equipped and trained for strategic offensive operations and incapable of providing national defence. Ukraine began its life as an independent state with a military establishment largely ignorant of the non-military dimension of security and imbued with the conviction that the danger of large-scale war was inherent in the international system. It also faced the burden of converting, privatising or dismantling a military-industrial complex of 1,840 enterprises, formerly producing almost 30 percent of the former Ukrainian Soviet Socialist Republic's GDP and organised on principles antithetical to the market. Most unhelpfully, the former USSR did bequeath to Ukraine a centralised (Union Republican) Ministry of Internal Affairs and KGB, the latter cross-bred with, and not only subordinate to, its All Union analogue, the KGB USSR, each of them with their own heavily militarised units established by the CPSU on the principle of 'divide and rule'. All of these establishments – centralised, compartmented and opaque – were subordinated to a scheme of 'civilian' (Party) control designed to confine authority and knowledge to very small circles of people. In the 1990s, it was against this template, not NATO's, that Ukraine's progress needed to be measured. Today that template no longer exists. But the pertinent question is whether a new one has taken shape that is cohesive, effective and sustainable.

Nevertheless, as the following pages substantiate, progress was unmistakable, and many of its defining thresholds were crossed before the Orange Revolution took place. From the collapse of the USSR, there were two impulses for positive change. The first was the necessity to transform *nezalezhnist'* (juridical independence) into *samostiynist'* (the 'ability to stand'). The relative absence of *samostiynist'* – the weakness of state and society, the alienation of ordinary people from the political order, the contradiction between 'European' aims and Soviet era (and increasingly criminalised) practices – had been identified by 1997 not only as barriers to Europe, but as threats to Ukraine's national security. Ukraine's official National Security Concept, drawn up by specialists from the National Security and Defence Council and ratified by the *Verkhovna Rada* in January that year, went so far as to define the 'strengthening of civil society' as the first of nine national security challenges. Yet during Kuchma's second term in office, the authorities succeeded in strengthening civil society less by design than by cynicism and misadventure. What they did accomplish, primarily during his first term, was essential and urgent: the construction of a state. The paradox confronting Ukraine today is that whilst civil society has developed enormously since 1997, and with renewed vigour after 2004, it now defines itself against the state authorities rather than in support of them. Whether they voted for Yanukovych, for Tymoshenko or did not vote at all, Ukrainians show every sign of agreeing with the judgement expressed by Oleksandr Goncharenko in 2001: that 'the principal threat to Ukraine is Ukraine itself'. Changing that perception is possibly President Yanukovych's greatest challenge.

The second impulse to change within the national security domain was the NATO-Ukraine relationship, launched when Ukraine joined Partnership for

Peace on 8 February 1994. Within a swift period of time, the scale and intensity of NATO-Ukraine cooperation became unprecedented in the Alliance's network of relationships with non-candidate states. Yet only after the signing of the Charter on a Distinctive Partnership at the Madrid Summit in July 1997 did that cooperation acquire a clear focus and direction, which then Minister of Defence Oleksandr Kuzmuk defined in October 2000 as 'supporting defence reform in the country'. By the time Kuchma left office, a significant measure of defence reform had been accomplished through several distinctive mechanisms (notably the Joint Working Group on Defence Reform) that provided structured audit and consultation, growing transparency and, despite the worsening political climate, a visible cultural change in the defence sector. It is indicative of these changes that the State Programme of Armed Forces Reform and Development 2001-2005 was submitted to NATO Headquarters for review at the same time as it was submitted to President Kuchma.

Nevertheless, the political climate did worsen in ways that flatly contradicted the core objectives officially proclaimed by NATO and Ukraine—and codified in the NATO-Ukraine Action Plan of 22 November 2002. Section I, almost half of that document, focused on political and economic issues, the better part of these directed towards entrenching democratic values and transforming *domestic* institutions and practices. The message was clear: it is the country, not the army that joins NATO, and the state of the country would be the principal benchmark that NATO would use to assess progress. It still is, and that approach is warmly endorsed by the authors of this volume.

Transformation and Disappointment

Many will wish to ponder why the starting conditions faced by Ukraine's post-Soviet establishment proved easier to surmount than those encountered by the country's democratically minded leaders fourteen years after Ukraine's independence had become an accomplished fact. Viktor Yushchenko's personal shortcomings and the corporate incapacity of his 'dear friends' and supporters have been the object of well deserved scrutiny. But that scrutiny begs the question of how realistic it would have been for any set of Ukrainian leaders to bring the country into the Europe of the twenty-first century. After 2005 President Yushchenko was not presented with the economically hollowed out Communist system that collapsed in Central Europe in 1989, but a far more resilient system of insider, illiberal capitalism that had matured, enriched itself and insinuated itself into the mentality of the state and the micro-sociology of life. Even had he possessed the mettle to battle with these conditions rather than succumb to them, it is highly debateable whether the policymaking elite and the country as a whole would have had the wherewithal to overcome them in the timescales demanded. As I wrote in a memo to the British government and NATO Headquarters in January 2005:

The powers [of the post-Soviet system] might be hated, but they are supple, adaptable, not easily outmanoeuvred and not readily dispensed with. Mistakes (and simple inertia) will be exploited not only by those who wish to capture the Orange revolution, but by those who wish to derail it—and possibly by those in Russia who want it to fail. Yushchenko's failure as president—which will be total if the electorate concludes that 'they have deceived us again'—will have far more serious consequences than Yushchenko's failure as a presidential candidate would have had.[1]

Despite these starting conditions—and in partial refutation of this grim forecast— the Orange leadership consolidated a transformation from virtual democracy to immature democracy. It presided over a considerable differentiation and maturation of elites in business as well as politics and greatly widened the ranks of those who understood the benefits of Euro-Atlantic standards and appreciated the distance Ukraine had to travel in order to turn them to tangible effect. Not least of all, it decisively shifted reform of the Armed Forces from the sphere of state documents to implementation. The significance of the State Programme of Armed Forces Development from 2006-2011 lay less in its radicalism than in measures which persuaded the army and Ukraine's partners that its ambitions—including the reduction of the military establishment from 260,000 to 143,000 and the provision of Joint Rapid Reaction Forces and Immediate Response Forces—were feasible and that they were being advanced. Such was the impact of measures undertaken by the team under Minister of Defence Anatoliy Grytsenko that NATO Headquarters regarded MAP for Ukraine as a 'done deal' until Viktor Yanukovych returned to power as Prime Minister in July 2006 and demanded a 'pause' in the process. Yet elsewhere, the reformist impulse was qualified, thwarted or absent.

In the security sector and law enforcement, the record has been decidedly mixed. That is hardly surprising. Unlike the services that make up the security sector, it was always possible for the Armed Forces to avoid becoming a component of internal political struggle. The roles of the latter are to defend state sovereignty and territorial integrity, insulate the country from external conflicts and, in the worst case, defend the country against external opponents. In contrast, the military and civilian components of the SBU, the Ministry of Internal Affairs (MVS) and, of course, *militsia* are on the cutting edge of the relationship between state and society, the law and the criminal, and hence they are subject to all of the strains and distortions inherent in these relationships. It is not remarkable that amateurism trumped the spirit of reform in the MVS or,

---

1 James Sherr, 'NATO/Allied Assistance to Ukraine'. Unpublished memo, 31 January 2005.

for all the activity of Minister Yuriy Lutsenko, objectives, structures and resources remained out of balance. If the *militsioner's* wages are inconsistent with life, it is inevitable that he will cheat (or steal) rather than die. That reality is as much in evidence today as it was in 2005. Fortunately for the Orange leaders, the most perilous work in changing the ethos of the SBU was accomplished by Ihor Smeshko between his appointment in September 2003 and his dismissal by President Yushchenko in February 2005. Fortunately for Ukraine, the service, not to say President Kuchma himself, constrained those determined to disperse the crowds on the *Maidan* by forceful means. Yet only in 2006 did two chairmen, Ihor Drizhchanyy and Valentyn Nalyvaychenko consolidate the service's 'de-KGBisation', uprooting the 'all Union' ethos of the KGB UkSSR and severing its successor's illicit ties with the KGB's Russian successors. Nevertheless, as the authors of this volume note, outside its headquarters on Volodymyrska, the 'democratisation' of this service has advanced at a far less satisfactory pace.

Second, corruption lost its harder edge and coercive component, but it has remained the dispiriting and defining reality of life. The Orange leaders either forgot or never properly grasped that crowds froze on the *Maidan* not in order that Ukraine should finally enter the EU (let alone NATO), but so that it would finally have leaders who governed in the country's interests rather than their own. This deficiency of leadership reflects political and sociological factors as well as personal ones. For one thing, the Orange leaders could not have come to power with the assistance of an ideologically diverse coalition and the support of forces within the country's powerful and resourceful state apparatus. They were also assisted by money, the donors of which not only had principled aspirations, but concrete interests. Moreover, for all their expressed repugnance towards the culture of power that arose in the Kuchma years, President Yushchenko, Prime Minister Tymoshenko and many of their closest allies built their careers inside it. The new leadership, therefore, exercised power with many of the forces, instruments and instincts of the old. It represented a principled break from the past, but not a clean break. In time, the principles mellowed.

Third, the Orange leaders failed to overhaul Ukraine's deeply flawed legal system. Instead, they sought to utilise it. Law in Communist and post-Communist states has rightly been called a system of 'codified arbitrariness'.[2] When Kuchma was in power, the law became a charter of harassment for every power in the land. It created a universe of petty offences, it withdrew two rights for every right given, it taxed new businesses before they earned their first kopeck, it nullified contracts at the drop of a hat, and it left everyone confused about what was permitted and what was forbidden. For those who were well

2 As characterised by the French authority on Russia and the Soviet Union, Françoise Thom.

connected (or able to pay), the legal order was negotiable. For everyone else, it was intolerable. The principal antidotes, *kriyshi* (shelters) from shadow structures or 'understandings' with the authorities, lay well outside the law. The demand to 'respect the law' is therefore double edged: by some, an earnest appeal against the capricious actions of self-serving authorities; by others a principled defence of the status quo's indefensible abuses and by still more, a weapon against rivals in business and politics. How can reform advance within this legal system? How can legality be maintained outside it? The new authorities eliminated the worst abuses and lightened a number of burdens. But they made no serious attempt to confront this dilemma.

Fourth, whilst the administrative culture of Ukraine in some spheres changed for the better, for the most part it remained unchanged, and in some critical spheres it regressed. The architects of Ukraine's system of national security had a weak national tradition, but they had a strong state tradition, and this was displayed in Horbulin's NSDC, which swiftly became a repository and incubator of professionalism. Lacking this tradition, Yushchenko transformed the NSDC from a public institution into a personal fiefdom, and the result has been a steady depletion of motivated professionals (though it must be said that his last appointee as Secretary, Raisa Bohatyreva has partially reversed this trend).

What the country sorely needs is institutionalisation: the process whereby rules not only establish authority and a basis for action, but also checks on authority, mechanisms of internal oversight and a normative framework that outlasts the tenure of office holders. For the most part, Ukraine's administrative staffs are not civil servants on the Western model, but state functionaries still largely schooled in the habits of Soviet bureaucracy: servility, rigid adherence to the most petty regulation, lack of regard for the opinions and feelings of subordinates, complete dependence on instructions, an incapacity to make decisions independently and a total lack of interest in the effect of their actions on ordinary people. At times, these functionaries exhibit the characteristics of their worst Western counterparts: evasion, concealment, duplicity, 'working to rule' and disdain for ideas 'not invented here'. But they have been given little incentive to cultivate the attributes that Western civil servants also exhibit: professional pride, standards of rightful conduct, initiative, teamwork, and an ethos of public responsibility.

Finally, the Orange authorities failed to see that this catalogue of missteps and steps not taken has national security implications:

- A rent-seeking local government and bureaucracy that does not allow legal entrepreneurship to flourish will not establish the conditions of fairness and trust that enable taxes to be paid and essential services (armed forces, police and bureaucracy itself) to be adequately funded by the state;

- Those who live in dread of *kompromat* (incriminating information) are equally likely to live in dread of transparency: the ability to know what decisions are taken, where they are taken, by whom they are taken or why. These habits of concealment make it difficult to ensure that resources are allocated as intended, identify and curb the role of intermediaries between buyer and seller, establish who owns Ukrainian enterprises as well as the connection between these owners, official structures and foreign countries. Without the mechanisms and data that produce transparency, it is also exceedingly difficult to discern which actors, domestic and foreign, influence the strategic direction of the economy and state.
- Those who treat information as a form of power rather than a public good will not only be dysfunctional administrators; they will hinder the timely sharing of information with those better able to assess it and utilise it than themselves. Defence against today's unconventional threats depends upon mid-level and sub-unit competence, the delegation of authority and, above all, the horizontal ('joined up') integration of agencies, branches and departments.
- Those whose business model is built upon deal making, cronyism and collusion with the state will not be able to advance integration into the competitive, rules based EU system even if they wish to do so.

Regression, Advance or Stalemate ?

For nineteen years Ukraine has defined itself unequivocally as a European rather than a Eurasian state. After the presidential elections of 17 January/7 February 2010, some fear that this era is drawing to a close. Many more fear that President Yanukovych will resurrect the hard corruption of the Kuchma era and reverse the democratisation that taken place over the last five years.

Yet these fears must be set in the context of six indisputable realities. The first is the secular transformation of Ukrainian society: intrinsically pluralistic, instinctively distrustful of power, civically active and increasingly self-reliant. Ukraine's electorate voted for stability rather than repression, and the polity is far from defenceless. The second is the fact that in order to use power effectively, Yanukovych will have to share it. He has not been elected by an absolute majority, but by a narrow plurality of voters who, with too many missteps by their leaders, could find themselves returned to minority status in short order. Without a broad parliamentary coalition, including former Yushchenko supporters, Yanukovych's appointees will not be confirmed, and many of his strategic initiatives will be stillborn. As leader of the opposition, Yulia Tymoshenko will do what she does best: become the guardian of Ukrainian patriotism and mobilise the disaffected. The third reality is the diversity of the Party of Regions itself: a party underwritten and influenced by a number of prominent individuals who have no wish to see Ukraine put additional barriers between itself and Europe. The fourth, amplified by the economic crisis, is that Western influence—and the influence of Western dominated financial institutions—has become inescapable. The fifth is that off the campaign trail, Yanukovych has shown no more desire to be a 'vassal of Russia' than his former patron, Leonid Kuchma. The sixth reality is that Russia has changed far less than Ukraine. Twelve days before Yanukovych's inauguration, President Medvedev's Head of Administration, Sergey Naryshkin, presented a list of demands to the incoming president, including the severance of intelligence cooperation with Western special services and the return of the FSB to Crimea.[3] This blunt and precipitate reinstitution of the practice of handing lists to presidents, so redolent of the Kuchma era, might accelerate Yanukovych's awakening to this reality as well as the other five.

The months that follow are likely to confirm the principle that whilst countries evolve, they do not reinvent themselves, let alone restore what they have lost. How Ukraine evolves remains an open question: for many to influence and for Ukrainians themselves to determine.

---

3 'Sweets à la Kyiv' [*Konfeta po-kievskiy*], *Kommersant-Vlast'*, 22 February 2010.

The Conceptual and Legal Bases of Ukraine's National Security

In contemporary political science there are two basic approaches to the understanding of the concept of 'national security'. Hans Morgenthau,[1] an American political scientist, defined national security as integrity of territory and institutes of the state. This approach emphasised military and political security, which is a traditional understanding of national security. Until now, this understanding prevailed in both the American and European discourse on security.

The second approach is *human security*. It has been characterised by a focus on not just military and political problems but economic, social, humanitarian and ecological ones too. The report by Chatham House can be viewed as a primary example of such an approach. It focuses on problems such as the AIDS epidemic, atypical pneumonia, the prevention and dealing with the consequences of man-made and national catastrophes, etc.[2] The second approach has become more prevalent in independent Ukraine.

Before turning to an analysis of the current legislation on national security, we will try to provide a brief summary of the views that have evolved from generations of Ukrainian lawmakers, including that of Ukrainian Soviet law experts.

Notwithstanding the fact that Ukraine enjoyed only nominal sovereignty, our interest in Soviet legislation has, above all, a practical character. The ideas and people that comprised the foundations of modern independent Ukraine developed within the Soviet context. To consider this question in a historical light it is necessary to define the sources of research. These include: the national laws at different stages of the development of Ukrainian statehood; relevant documents of political parties; memoirs of political state and public figures; works of historians; political scientists and legislators. These sources would certainly allow the systematic exploration of the question. At the same time, however, this method poses a recurring problem for a researcher: to avoid getting submerged in the 'information voices' of different periods and to select

---

1 Morgenthau, Hans & Kenneth Thompson, *Politics Among Nations*, 6th edition, New York: McGraw-Hill, 1985.

2 'Human Security and Resilience', Briefing Paper, Chatham House and the Economic & Social Research Council, February 2006.

the sources and research methods that would help elucidate the essence of the phenomena under consideration. In our opinion, this methodology is one of the principal occupations of political analysts, which the authors of this book are not.

Therefore, in order to analyse the political-legal models for ensuring the national security of Ukraine, the most appropriate sources to begin with are the constitutions, since 'constitutional norms are the criteria for the legitimisation of political processes and structures'.[3] In cases of necessity, other sources will be consulted to describe in detail the nature of the evolution of political-legal models for ensuring the national security of Ukraine.

The provisions of the various constitutions and constitutional acts of Ukraine contain interesting materials about the origins of political-legal ideas on the questions of national security and political decision making in this sphere during different historical periods of development of Ukrainian statehood in the 20th century. However, these acts of national legislation refer to the concept of 'national security' as a political-legal category for the first time in Article 1145 of the Constitution (Basic law) of the Ukrainian Soviet Socialist Republic (Ukrainian SSR) in 1978 with amendments introduced in September 1994. Therefore, in our analysis of previous constitutions and constitutional acts, we will look at the provisions that regulate legal relationships, which in contemporary political theory and practice relate to the sphere of national security, namely: the defence industry, international relations and internal security.

Worthy of note is the fact that the Ukrainian security sector went through a historically difficult and inconsistent development. Modern Ukrainian statehood originates in the 17th century with the Cossack army. In modern terms this implies martial law. The history of Het'manschyna is above all the history of the army and its territorial organisation. Even the administrative division of this Ukrainian political entity in the 17th-18th centuries corresponded to a military structure (regiments and hundreds). An interesting question for historical speculation (and indeed research) is: whether the organisation of Byzantium in the 8th 12th centuries influenced this administrative division, through the 'Kievan Rus' and the inherited traditions of the settled military estate (armour, boyars etc.), for example. Do similar conditions generate similar institutions? However, for the purpose of our study the answer to these questions is not significant.

We will focus instead on the development of the Ukrainian security sector in the 20th century, paying special attention to the constitutional-legal regulation of this sphere for the realisation of the functions of the state.

---

3 Politychnyy entsyklopedychnyy slovnyk, Yu.S. Shemshuchenko and V.D. Babkin (eds.), In-t derzhavy i prava im. V.M. Korets'koho NAN Ukrayiny, Ukrayins'ka asotsiatsiya politolohiv. Kyiv: Geneza, 1997, p. 167.

The 1918 Constitution of the Ukrainian People's Republic (UNR) 'The Statute on the Political System, Rights and Liberties of the Ukrainian People's Republic', adopted by the Central Council of the UNR on 28 April 1918, instituted a democratic political-legal model of the national security sector. In fact, the statute contains a constitutional stipulation about general principles in the formation of the armed forces (Article 46), according to which the call-up for mandatory 'military or militia service' is carried out in accordance with the decision of the National Assembly. According to the statute, the powers of the assembly also include the proclamation of war, approved by no less than two thirds of the present assembly.[4]

On internal security, chapter VIII of the statute contains principles, order and procedures for the temporary suspension of civil liberties 'during wartime or internal insurgency'. The suspension must take place on the basis of a special law adopted by the National Assembly and not continue for more than three months.[5]

The work of the UNR leadership in 1917–1918 was mockingly and perhaps unfairly depicted by Oleksandr Oles, a Ukrainian poet, in a well-known epigram: '... invited Germans to our corner, and took down the Central Council'. After the coup d'état, in April 1918, Hetman of all Ukraine Pavlo Skoropads'kyy, approved a 'Law on the Temporal Political System in Ukraine'. According to this document, exceptional powers were granted to the country's head of state in relation to national security. Specifically, the conduct of international relations (Article 4), armed forces (Article 5) and the announcement of 'martial law, blockades or emergency situations' in certain regions (Article 6). Article 12 proclaimed that 'defence of the Fatherland is the sacred duty of every Cossack and citizen of the Ukrainian state'.[6]

Pavlo Skoropads'kyy's contradictory policy largely led to the fall of the Ukrainian state as a result of an anti-Hetman revolt in November-December of 1918.

After coming to power, the UNR Directory also adopted legislation governing the activity of the security sector. Decisions taken by the Labour Congress in 1919 were in the same vein as the UNR statute. Article 2 of the 'Law on the Temporal Supreme Authority and the Legislation Procedure in the Ukrainian People's Republic', adopted by the Council of People's Ministers of the UNR on 12 November 1920, gave the head of the UNR Directory powers in the field of external relations; namely, approval of agreements with other states adopted by the State People's Council and representation of the UNR in

---

4 Konstytutsiyi i konstytutsiyni akty Ukrayiny, Yu.S. Shemshuchenko (ed.), Instytut derzhavy i prava im. V.M. Korets'koho NAN Ukrayiny. Kyiv, 2001, p. 55.

5 Ibid., p. 60.

6 Ibid., pp. 62–63.

relations with them.[7] These models, however, were never fully realised as a result of revolutionary unrest that culminated in the coming to power of the Bolsheviks in Ukraine.

The Constitution of the Ukrainian Soviet Socialist Republic (Ukrainian SSR) of 14 May 1919 laid the foundations for the long-term development of the totalitarian model of the national security sector. This constitution enshrined a more complex system for the adoption of political decisions made in the name of national security. It was based on a general thesis that the armed defence of 'socialist revolution' is one of the key tasks of the Ukrainian SSR on route to socialism through 'the dictatorship of working and exploited masses' (Articles 1, 2, 3d).

Relations with 'foreign states, the declaration of war and the achievement of agreements' (Article 6, Article 1c), as well as 'the bases for the organisation of armed forces' (Article 6, Article 1d), were defined as responsibilities of 'Central Soviet Power in Ukraine'. The latter had the following organs defined in Article 7 of the constitution: the All-Ukrainian Congress of Soviets of Workers'; Peasant and Red Army Deputies; the All-Ukrainian Central Executive Committee of Soviets (ACECS) and the Council of People's Commissars (CPC).

The adoption, introduction of changes and amendments to the constitution as well as the question of war and peace were defined as the prerogatives of the Congress of Soviets. However, in case of 'emergency and impossibility to convene the Congress in due time', the question of war and peace was delegated to ACECS (Articles 10 and 13). Article 29 determined principles of the formation of the armed forces on the basis of universal conscription of 'all working masses' and defined other military duties for the 'non-working elements'.

Other articles also had an explicitly discriminatory character concerning the 'non-working elements'. For example, seven categories of citizens were deprived of the right to vote and be elected (Article 21), and Article 33 provided for the right to deprive 'individuals and groups of political rights, if these rights are used against the Socialist revolution'.[8]

Political and social discrimination of citizens had de facto been happening for a long period and had been enshrined in law for almost sixty years, including in the Constitution of the Ukrainian SSR of 1919, which remained until the introduction of changes and amendments to the Constitution of the Ukrainian SSR of 1937 during the fourth session of the Verkhovna Rada of the Ukrainian SSR of the ninth convocation in 1977. In our view, it became perhaps the main reason and a permanent factor complicating

---

7 Konstytutsiyi i konstytutsiyni akty Ukrayiny, p. 79.

8 Konstytutsiyi i konstytutsiyni akty Ukrayiny, pp. 69–77.

the situation in the field of external and internal security during the Socialist period of Ukrainian statehood.

At the same time, one should not forget a considerable European influence on the interpretation of the concept *narod* (people). The Bolshevik-Leninists were guided, on the whole, by the formula 'people as the embodiment of sovereignty'. However, the notion of people included only 'the working masses' and omitted 'the exploiters'. In comparison with educational, property or residency qualifications of the European constitutional laws of the 19th century, the criterion of defining 'the people' changed. The principle of equating the population with the people remained. Further ideas on this topic can be found in the dissertation of a Kyivan researcher, Maksym Palamarchuk.[9]

A gradual erosion of control by Ukraine over its defence and internal security was reflected in the subsequent Soviet constitutions adopted after the formation of the Union of Soviet Socialist Republics.

The Constitution (Basic law) of the Ukrainian Soviet Socialist Republic,[10] adopted on 15 May 1929, is conceptually based on the principles laid down in the Constitution of the Ukrainian SSR in 1919. It explicitly sets out the limitations of state sovereignty (Article 3), particularly in the areas of external and internal security and defence, which occurred after the formation of the USSR. Except for the questions of the change of borders of the Ukrainian SSR, no other relevant powers were assigned to the All-Ukrainian Congress of Soviets (Article 22). As noted by certain Ukrainian researchers,[11] this is a reflection of the thorny and conflicting process involved in the determination of the state and the administrative borders of the union republics within the framework of the USSR.

In comparison with the powers of the All-Ukrainian Central Executive Committee (defined in the Constitution of the Ukrainian SSR of 1919), the powers of the All-Ukrainian Central Executive Committee (ACEC) in the field of defence were limited only to participation 'within the limits set in the legislation of the Union of Soviet Socialist Republics in the formation of the armed forces…' (Article 30).

Article 42 of the Constitution determined the number and composition of government institutions (12 people's commissariats), including the People's Commissariat of Internal Affairs. Article 43 stated that '*the State Political Administration of the Ukrainian Soviet Socialist Republic chaired by the person who simultaneously served as the representative of the United State Political Administration of the Union of Soviet Socialist Republics was responsible for the organisation of the fight against political and economic counterrevolution*'.

---

9 Palamarchuk M.O., Mekhanizmy realizatsiyi vlady narodu u konteksti zabezpechennya natsional'noyi bezpeky, Kyiv: NIPMB, 2007.

10 Ibid., pp. 83–130.

11 Serhiychuk V., Etnichni mezhi i derzhavnyy kordon Ukrayiny, Ternopil', 1996.

Article 15 declared universal conscription a principle of defence policy, retaining the discriminatory norm of Article 29 of the 1919 constitution on the 'non-working elements'.

The constitution of 1929, in contrast to the constitution of 1919, enhanced constitutional principles entailing political discrimination of certain groups of citizens. Article 67 retains the norms of Article 33 of the 1919 constitution concerning seven categories of citizens who are 'deprived of voting rights'. Whilst Article 33 of the 1919 constitution contained only a general declaration on this point, Article 68 moreover grants powers to a concrete executive body, ACEC, to define 'the categories of citizens deprived of voting rights'. The question as to how the ACEC used these powers is outside the scope of this study.

Attention is further required in respect to Article 13 of the 1929 constitution, which determines policy in respect of proletarian culture and a stipulation about the necessity for the state 'to resolutely fight nationalist prejudices'. However, by December 1929, stirred by the organs of the State Political Directorate (DPU) of Ukraine, a large group of prominent Ukrainian intellectuals was condemned in a public trial in Kharkiv for allegedly participating in a 'nationalist organisation'—'The Union for the Liberation of Ukraine'(SVU). Notwithstanding a usually contemptuous attitude toward the constitutions of Soviet Ukraine as mere window dressing, this incident proves quite a strong correlation between practical policies, including the repressive ones, of the state authorities and the basic laws of the Ukrainian SSR.

The authors could not find the corresponding analogies (to 'resolutely fight nationalist prejudices') in the constitution of the USSR or in the constitutions of some other union republics at the end of the 1920s and early 1930s. In particular, the Constitution of the Russian SFSR of 1925[12], the Constitution of the Uzbek SSR of 1931[13] and the Constitutions of the Byelorussian RSR of 1927[14] did not contain any such stipulation.

Is it perhaps an original and inherently Ukrainian political, cultural and constitutional-legal phenomenon? In that case, we should analyse the reasons that brought the phenomenon to life. Perhaps the Ukrainian 'nationalist danger' was perceived by the political leadership of the Ukrainian SSR and the USSR in accordance with the historical logic of the political system and course selected by them. What factors might be considered? In the author's view, there are several.

---

12 'Konstitutsiya i konstitutsionnyye akty RSFSR. 1918–1937', in Sbornik dokumentov pod obshhey redaktsyyey akademika A.Y. Vyshynskogo. Moscow: Izdvo 'Vedomostey Verkhovnogo Soveta RSFSR', 1940, pp. 162–171.

13 Konstitutsiya (Osnovnoy Zakon) Uzbekskoy Sovetskoy Sotsialisticheskoy Respubliki, Tashkent: Izdvo SNK, 1932.

14 Konstytutsiya BRSR, Mins'k: Vydvo CEC BRSR, 1927.

First, the high ranking Soviet functionaries assumed that a permanent danger existed from the outside. It therefore assumed a nationalist overtone as there had been a large Ukrainian emigration, outnumbered only by the Russian one. These political refugees found themselves abroad as a result of the civil war that raged from 1918-1921 but did not abandon their attempts to fight for the independence of the Ukrainian state by political or other means.

Second, and possibly the main source of internal threats, was the former pre-revolutionary Ukrainian intelligentsia. They were the true defenders of the ideas and traditions of European democracy and political pluralism in general and in questions of nation and state were representatives of a modern urban Ukraine. In the author's opinion, it was precisely these circumstances that necessitated the 'SVU' process, initiated by the Soviet power and defined its public character and the composition of the process 'participants'.

The Constitution (Basic Law) of the Ukrainian Soviet Socialist Republic of 30 January 1937[15] entrenched the ultimate loss of state sovereignty in the management of external relations and defence. In accordance with Article 13 of the Constitution of the Ukrainian SSR and Article 14 of the Constitution of the USSR, it delegated these functions to the high bodies of power and state administration of the USSR. Interestingly, for example, the powers of the Ukrainian authorities defined in the constitution of 1929—with regard to the change of the borders of the Ukrainian SSR—were replaced with the powers 'to define the borders and regional divisions of the Ukrainian SSR' (Article 19) in the 1937 constitution. In the field of security, the same article defined the powers of the Ukrainian SSR with regard to 'the protection of the political system and citizens rights'. In the field of internal security, the powers of the executive power—the Council of People's Commissars of the Ukrainian SSR—included taking measures to 'defend the social system, defence interests of the state and citizens rights' (Article 43).

In the Constitution of the Ukrainian SSR of 1937, the process of centralisation of the key functions of state administration within the framework of the USSR became evident, in particular in the field of internal security: The People's Commissariat for Internal Affairs (NKVS) was transferred to the union-republican level (Article 48), and at the same time its head was to be a member of government—the Council of People's Commissars of the Ukrainian SSR (Article 45). In this context, a typical example is that regional soviets, having obtained the right to form the departments in their executive committees (Article 87) identical in function and title to those of the Council of People's Commissars of the Ukrainian SSR (Article 45), were limited in this right in relation to NKVS. Article 88 determines that NKVS forms its departments in regional soviets. Article 131 pronounces a universal military

15 Konstytutsiyi i konstytutsiyni akty Ukrayiny, pp. 104–130.

duty and calls military service in the Workers'-Peasant Red Army 'a duty of honour of citizens of the Ukrainian SSR'.

In the constitution of 1937, the stipulations of the previous constitutions of 1919 and 1929 regarding discrimination of citizens on socio-political grounds were eliminated. Only 'mentally-ill persons and persons convicted by courts' (Article 134) were deprived of their voting rights. At the same time, it needs to be stressed that disenfranchising people became almost a permanent practice of the courts in the Ukrainian SSR from 1930–1940.

Perhaps for the first time, actors and other sources of threat to public and state security were defined at the constitutional level. The notorious term 'the enemy of the people', coined during the Great French Revolution, made its appearance in the Constitution of the Ukrainian SSR of 1937. Article 130 stipulated: '...persons who encroach upon the communal and socialist property are the enemies of the people'. In contrast with the constitution of 1929, which delegated the task of the fight against 'nationalist superstitions' to the state, there is a new term in the constitution of 1937—'nationalist counterrevolution' (Article 2).

It is possible to consider as innovative the fact that the constitution of 1937 contained the norms of criminal law and identified as treasonable offences the violation of oath, defection to the enemy, infliction of damage upon the military power of the state and espionage (Article 132).

The law also defined constitutional preconditions that enabled the Communist Party (Bolsheviks of Ukraine), which 'is a leading element of all organisations of workers, both civil and state ones' (Article 125), to dominate the political system.

The Constitution of the Ukrainian Soviet Socialist Republic of 30 January 1937, with amendments and additions was introduced at the fourth session of the Verkhovna Rada of the ninth convocation in 1977.[16] It contained a number of stipulations, lost as a result of the adoption of the constitution in 1937. These related to the restoration of some sovereignty to Ukrainian SSR in external relations and defence. In particular, the Ukrainian SSR obtained the right to have its own republican military formations (Article 15a) as well as 'to establish direct contacts with foreign states, conclude agreements with them and exchange diplomatic and consular representatives' (Article 15b).

The last development occurred on 1 February 1944 and was defined, according to some researchers, by the desire of the USSR leadership in post-war time 'to increase the number of states which would be able to take part in the work of the United Nations Organisation, where every voice in deciding the fate of the world was crucial'.[17]

---

16 Ibid., p. 131–155.

17 Ovsiy I.V., Zovnishnya polityka Ukrayiny (vid davnikh chasiv do 1944 roku), Kyiv: Lybid', 2002, p. 218.

In accordance with the constitution of 1977, the Presidium of the Verkhovna Rada of the Ukrainian SSR had powers in external relations on the nomination and recall of representatives of the Ukrainian SSR in foreign states as well as of foreign states in the Ukrainian SSR (Article 30). The Council of Ministers of the Ukrainian SSR had powers to 'manage the field of external relations of the Ukrainian SSR with foreign states on the basis of a general procedure established in the USSR on relations of union republics with foreign states' (Article 43h). This function was executed directly by the All-Union Ministry of Foreign Affairs (Article 48).

The Ukrainian SSR had powers to establish the procedure for the formation of the army of the Ukrainian SSR (Article 19). The Council of Ministers of the Ukrainian SSR had powers to 'manage the creation of the armed formations' (Article of 43g). In the list of the All-Union Ministries, the Ministry of Defence was included (Article 48). Incidentally, the first and only Minister of Defence of the Ukrainian SSR was the commander of the troops of the Kyivan territorial district, General-Lieutenant V. Herasymenko. A stipulation on general military duty was also included (Article 112).

The chairman of the Committee of State Security at the Council of Ministers of the Ukrainian SSR was a member of the Council of Ministers (Article 45). The Ministry of Internal Affairs had the status of the All-Union Ministry (Article 48). The constitution of 1977 retained a number of stipulations from the constitution of 1937, namely 'nationalist counterrevolution' (Article 2), 'enemies of the people' (Article 111) as well as concrete norms of criminal law on crimes such as high treason (Article 113).

The number of categories of citizens who were deprived of the right to vote was greatly reduced. Only mentally ill people were categorised 'in accordance with the procedure established in the law' (Article 115).

As in the constitution of 1937, the leading role of the Communist Party of the Soviet Union in the political system of the state was laid down in Article 106.

The Constitution (Basic Law) of the Ukrainian Soviet Socialist Republic, adopted during the extraordinary seventh session of the Verkhovna Rada of the Ukrainian SSR of the ninth convocation in 1978, addressed the question of national security in chapter 4 'Foreign Policy Activity and Protection of the Socialist Motherland' (Articles 28–30). It stressed that the Ukrainian SSR is guided in its foreign policy activity by the aims, tasks and principles of foreign policy defined in the Constitution of the USSR. It takes part in ensuring security and defence capacity of the country, equipment of the armed forces of the USSR, etc. A stipulation on general military duty is retained. Powers and duties of organs of power and civil organisations of the Ukrainian SSR in ensuring the security and defence capacity of the country are determined in the legislation of the USSR.

Accordingly, the constitution of 1978 delegates responsibility for representation in international relations to the highest organs of power and management of the Ukrainian SSR (Article 72). Thus the Presidium of the Verkhovna Rada of the Ukrainian SSR is responsible for ratification and denunciation of international agreements, the nomination and recall of representatives of the Ukrainian SSR as well as acceptance and recall of credentials of diplomatic representatives of foreign states (Article 108). Management of the field of international relations, as underlined, 'in accordance with the procedure established by the USSR', is delegated to the Council of Ministers (CM) of the Ukrainian SSR (Article 118).

In the same article, the Council of Ministers of the Ukrainian SSR is responsible for taking measures, 'within the limits set in the Constitution of the USSR, in ensuring security and defence capacity of the country'. The notion of 'state security' was used for the first time in the Constitution of the Ukrainian SSR of 1978.

A particular feature of the constitution of 1978 was that the direct norms of criminal law concerning crimes such as high treason were eliminated (Article 60). The term 'enemies of the people' was also eliminated, however, the article on socialist property (Article 59) was retained. In content, it was analogous to Article 130 of the constitution of 1937 and Article 111 of the Constitution of the Ukrainian SSR of 1977.

Article 6 clearly defined the leading role of the Communist Party of the Soviet Union in the political system of the Soviet society. The term 'nationalist counterrevolution' from Article 2 of the Constitution of the Ukrainian SSR of 1937 also experienced some modifications. It was defined in Article 2 of the Constitution of the Ukrainian SSR of 1978 as 'bourgeois-nationalist counterrevolution'.

The problematic and conflicting circumstances related to the renewal of sovereignty of the Ukrainian state have been studied comprehensively in national and foreign literature and detailed in the memoirs of renowned figures. However, focusing on the research that exists, it is necessary to refer to the example of the Law 'On the List of Ministries and other Central Organs of State Administration of the Ukrainian SSR', adopted by the Verkhovna Rada of the Ukrainian SSR on 13 May 1991. This law named only the Ministry of Internal Affairs among the organs responsible for management of the security sector. Article 2 of this law highlighted a distinctive status to the KGB of the Ukrainian SSR that did not fall under the jurisdiction of the latter's Council of Ministers. This may be explained as the result of pressure from Moscow on the leadership of Ukraine at that time. According to the Law 'On Ministries and State Committees of the Ukrainian SSR' (adopted on 3 August 1990), the KGB of the Ukrainian SSR fell under the jurisdiction of the Ukrainian government.

We should note that this law was adopted about two weeks after the adoption of the Declaration of State Sovereignty of Ukraine.

Ukraine's aspirations to the restoration of its sovereignty were realised by the Declaration of State Sovereignty of Ukraine adopted by the Verkhovna Rada of the Ukrainian SSR on 16 July 1990 (chapter III). The declaration also included sovereignty over the area of international relations, security and defence.

In particular, chapter X entitled 'External Relations' stated that on the subject of international law, the Ukrainian SSR engages in direct relations in the fulfilment of the goal of 'effectively providing for national interests of the Republic'. The concept 'national interests' was used for the first time in this constitutional act. Chapter X proclaimed the duty to support the strengthening of peace and international security through participation in the European process and structures.

Chapter XI entitled 'External and Internal Security' declared the right of Ukraine to possess its own armed and internal forces. It defined general approaches on the procedure for carrying out military service, and in particular the prohibition to deploy citizens of Ukraine on active military service outside Ukraine without the consent of the Verkhovna Rada. It also proclaimed the intention of Ukraine becoming a permanently neutral state in the future, not taking part in military blocks and to adhere to the three non-nuclear principles.

The Declaration of State Sovereignty of Ukraine contains a section entitled 'Ecological Security', chapter VII, which highlights the acuteness of this problem for Ukraine, particularly in light of the impact of the Chernobyl (atomic station) Disaster in 1986.

One of priorities in the field of national security was defence of the national statehood (chapter I 'The Self-Determination of the Ukrainian Nation'). The final positions noted that the principles of the declaration would be applied during the conclusion of a new union treaty of the USSR Republics.

Finally, we would like to stress that notwithstanding a considerable tradition of statehood in Ukraine, there were no appropriate institutions, traditions and staff able to create a modern management system for the national security sector at the strategic level when it became independent. At the beginning of 1992 there were only three experts in Ukraine in the field of military sciences (doctors of sciences). However, none of them was acquainted with the questions of strategic management.

The situation among the members of parliament, governmental officials, employees of the state security organs in scientific and research organisations, and among politicians was no better. Of the forty seven political parties that existed in Ukraine in 1997, only seven managed to semi-professionally outline in their manifestos their policies in the field of national security.

That said, justice must be done to the political leadership of Ukraine during the period of the 1990s. It clearly understood the value of the sphere of national security in the affirmation of Ukraine's independence. In this period, a number of urgent measures were carried out on the formation of a system of strategic management in 'national security'. On the whole, Ukrainian legislators opted for human security with its broader approach to the understanding of the concept of national security. This was to form a powerful legal base for national security policies during Ukraine's seventeen years of independence. In chronologic order, the stages by which this base was formed appear thus:

On 18 April 1991, the Verkhovna Rada of the Ukrainian SSR, restoring the European traditions of the Ukrainian People's Republic of the period of 1918–1919, formed the Cabinet of Ministers and introduced the positions of 'state ministers' with the purpose of improving the 'state management structure'. Corresponding changes to the constitution in place at that time were introduced on 21 May 1991.

On 24 April 1991, the Verkhovna Rada of the Ukrainian SSR changed the title of the Parliamentary Commission on External and Internal Security to 'The Commission of the Verkhovna Rada of the Ukrainian SSR on Defence and State Security'. On the same day, twenty seven members of the commission chaired by V. Dyrdynets' were elected.

Between May 21 and June 5th, 1991, seven state ministers of the Ukrainian SSR were appointed. Among them, two public officials, the state minister for defence, state security and emergency situations (Y. Marchuk) and the state minister for the defence complex and conversion (V. Antonov), were directly responsible for the sphere of security. Worthy of note is the fact that at that time there were already twenty-two central organs of executive power (ministries) in Ukraine.

On 24 August 1991, the Act of Declaration of Independence of Ukraine was proclaimed. All military formations deployed on the Ukrainian territory became answerable to the Parliament of Ukraine. The Ministry of Defence of Ukraine was created on the basis of the management organs of the Kyiv military district. The creation of the Armed Forces of Ukraine had begun.

On 24 August 1991, a number of other strategic decisions were adopted, including the formation of the Defence Council of Ukraine (Decision of the Verkhovna Rada of Ukraine 'On the Political Situation in Ukraine and Immediate Actions of the Verkhovna Rada of Ukraine on the Creation of Conditions for Prevention in the Future of a Military Coup'). On 3 September 1991, K. Morozov was appointed the minister of defence of Ukraine. On 20 September 1991, the National Security Service of Ukraine was formed. In December 1991, L. Kravchuk was elected as the president of Ukraine. One of his first decisions was the formation of the National Security and Defence Council of Ukraine (Decree 41/92 of 15 January 1992).

By September 1994, some amendments had been made to the 1978 Constitution of Ukraine. These new provisions set in place some of the principles for the construction of a national security system (in particular, the distribution of competencies in this sphere among the branches of power). Those principles were further developed in the constitutional agreement in 1995.

Therefore, chapter X entitled 'External Relations and the Defence of the Motherland' contains a norm, specifically, Article 30, which states that 'the duties of state organs, civil organisations, state officials and citizens in ensuring the security of the country and strengthening its defence capacity are determined in the legislation of Ukraine'.

The distribution of power among the various branches within the field of national security was defined as follows in the constitution. The Verkhovna Rada of Ukraine (Article 97) has exceptional powers to decide on the questions related to the change of state borders of Ukraine and the determination of the key directions of domestic and foreign policies. It forms the National Defence Council of Ukraine and defines its composition, nominates the chairman of the National Security Service of Ukraine, approves the candidates for the positions of the ministers for foreign affairs, defence and internal affairs, the chairman of the State Committee on Protection of the State Border as well as the chairman of the State Customs Committee proposed by the president of Ukraine. It decides on the question of ecological security, about the opening of diplomatic and trade representation offices of Ukraine, the ratification and denunciation of international agreements as well as the introduction of the state of emergency in Ukraine. The parliament approves the decrees of the president of Ukraine about the declaration of war as well as the introduction of military and emergency situations.

The president of Ukraine, as head of state and the executive branch of power (Article 114–1), in accordance with Article 114–5, serves as the guarantor of the rights and freedoms of citizens, state sovereignty of Ukraine and represents Ukraine in its international relations. He is the commander-in-chief of the Armed Forces of Ukraine and takes measures aimed at the provision of the state's defence capacity, national security and territorial integrity. He has the right to negotiate and sign intergovernmental and international agreements of Ukraine with their subsequent ratification by the parliament, appoint and recall diplomatic representatives of Ukraine in other states and accordingly legitimise the representatives of foreign states in Ukraine. The other considerable powers of the president include the announcement of war, introduction of martial law, general or partial mobilisation in case of an armed attack, introduction of the state of emergency and announcement of extraordinary ecological situations in certain regions.

The same article of the constitution determines specific mechanisms of cooperation between the Verkhovna Rada and the president of Ukraine as part of the annual and extraordinary messages of the president of Ukraine. In particular, this message relates to the situation in Ukraine and the program of internal and foreign policies of the president and the government of Ukraine.

Principles and policy directions in relation to ecological security (chapter VII), external and internal security (chapter IX) as well as international relations (chapter X), set in the Declaration of State Sovereignty of Ukraine in 1991, were reconfirmed in the constitution.

The principle of protection of national statehood (Article 7), proclaimed in the Declaration of State Sovereignty of Ukraine, was extended and entrenched. According to this principle, the creation and activity of parties, other civil organisations and movements, which pursue the goal of 'changing the constitutional system by violence and encroaching upon the territorial integrity of the state in any illegal form as well as disrupting its security and instigating national and religious animosity' is prohibited.

In relation to basic principles for the organisation and functioning of self-government in the interim and until the adoption of a new constitution, the Verkhovna Rada and the president of Ukraine, via the constitutional agreement of 8 June 1995, introduced some changes. These were namely to the control that the branches of power within national security and defence possessed and were in contrast with the previous constitution.

Specifically, the Verkhovna Rada (Article 17) was given new responsibility in human rights protection, the establishment of a general structure and composition of the armed forces, border troops, the National Guard, troops of the Security Service of Ukraine and other military formations.

Article 18 contains a stipulation whereby only laws can determine the principles of domestic and external policy, defence and state security, protection of the environment and the status of foreign troops in Ukrainian territory. It also sets down the procedures for the use of the armed forces outside Ukraine, the legal norms on the state border on martial law and the state of emergency.

The president of Ukraine, as the commander-in-chief of the armed forces (Article 24), has the right to appoint and dismiss the forces' 'high command'. He is also the chairman of a new state organ relating to national security—the National Defence Council of Ukraine—and possesses the right to nominate those who will sit on it. Thus, this advisory and coordinating structure in the system of the presidential branch of power in Ukraine, created by presidential decree in 1992, obtained constitutional status. The same article grants to the president the right to take decisions about the recognition of foreign states in international relations. The powers of the government in the field of national security did not change substantially.

The constitution of Ukraine adopted by the Verkhovna Rada of Ukraine on 28 June 1996 defined the main principles of the existing political and legal model for the provision of national security and the authority of the branches of power in this sphere.

The main political principles are defined within the chapter on 'General Provisions'. Namely, the Ukrainian State is sovereign, democratic and based on the rule of law (Article 1) and that that the principles of supremacy of law (Article 8) and human rights (Article 3) are recognised as the highest social values. At the same time, a number of human rights, specifically, the right to inviolability of privacy (Article 32), freedom of thought and speech (Article 34), freedom of association with political parties and civil organisations (Article 36) and the right to hold meetings, marches and demonstrations (Article 39) can be limited in accordance with the procedures set down in the law in the interests of national security.

In accordance with the constitution, the state cannot impose any single ideology; the freedom of political activity is guaranteed (Article 15) and depolitisation of state administration is set as the norm in Article 37. This forbids the formation and activity of organised politics within the organs of executive and judicial power, executive local self-governing bodies, state enterprises and within educational establishments. The same article forbids the formation and activity of political parties and civil society associations whose programs or activities are directed at:

> *The liquidation of independence of Ukraine, change of the constitutional system by force, violation of sovereignty and territorial integrity of the state, violation of its security, illegal overthrow of the state authorities, propaganda of war, violence, instigation of inter-ethnic, racial and religious animosity, encroachment upon the rights and freedoms of a person.*

Political-legal priorities for ensuring national security, including territorial integrity and inviolability, sovereignty and the constitutional system of Ukraine (Articles 2 and 17), ecological (Article 16), economic, information and state security as well as the defence of the state border (Article 17) are also defined.

However, the primary legal base for managing national security is Article 17 of the constitution, which was not changed in any of the constitutional drafts developed between 2003 and 2008. This article stipulates:

> *The protection of the sovereignty and territorial indivisibility of Ukraine, and ensuring the State's economic and information security are the most important functions of the State and of the utmost concern for all Ukrainians.*
> *Defence, the protection of sovereignty, territorial indivisibility and inviolability of Ukraine, are entrusted to the Armed Forces.*

> *State Security and border protection are entrusted to the respective State Military and Law Enforcement Organisations, whose operational procedures are stipulated by law.*
> *The Armed Forces and other State Military Organisations shall not be usurped to restrict the rights and freedoms of citizens or used to overthrow the constitutional order, subvert the bodies of power or obstruct their activities.*
> *The State ensures the social protection of citizens of Ukraine who serve in the Armed Forces and in other State Military Organisations as well as members of their families. The creation and operation of paramilitary organisations or groups not pre-determined by law are prohibited in Ukraine.*
> *The positioning of foreign military bases shall not be permitted in Ukraine.*

It is impossible to argue with the view of Ukrainian human rights defender Y. Zakharov.[18] His critique relates to the general shortcomings of this article's construction and its many contradictions. In particular, this assessment is levelled at a paradoxical situation where the state, the Ukrainian people and the Armed Forces are all made responsible for the protection of sovereignty and territorial integrity.

The second part of the article purposefully limits the number of groups involved in ensuring the defence of Ukraine, i.e. only the Armed Forces. Yet in fact the president, the Cabinet, central and local organs of power as well as the Security Service of Ukraine, intelligence bodies and the Ministry of Internal Affairs take an active part in the implementation of these tasks within the limits of their jurisdiction.

In Section 3 of Article 17 the anachronistic concept of 'state security' is used. However, the substance of the article embraces the concept of 'national security'. The term 'state security' is a throwback from the Soviet era. The latter term is partly connected with the several meanings of the word 'national' in English, which means both nation and state. It should also be mentioned that presently the concept of 'state security' is used mainly by authoritarian regimes, such as the People's Republic of China.

The same article prohibits the demilitarisation of the special services, above all of intelligence bodies, and entrusts state security exclusively to military formations and law enforcement bodies.

Part 4 of this article prohibits the use of the Armed Forces or any other military formations for the limitation of the rights and freedoms of its citizens. Its effect is to deny the existence of the Internal Troops of the Ministry of Internal Affairs, which causes serious problems for the day-to-day functioning of the intelligence bodies as well as the Security Service of Ukraine. It also entirely deprives the Armed Forces of their so called internal function. Given

---

18 Zakharov, Y., Khto napyshe novu Konstytutsiyu Ukrayiny, http://maidan.org.ua/static/mai/1213204674.html

the present level of threats and challenges to national security and the development of society this is, at best, paradoxical.

In the face of these contradictions, we consider it necessary to begin a consultation with experts in the field of national security and constitutional law with a view to modernising Article 17 of the constitution and abandoning the declarative form adopted in the newest version of this article as well as the constitution as a whole.

The 1996 constitution defines the jurisdiction and powers of the branches of power in the field of national security. This question and the problems that emerged later are considered in detail in chapter 5.

Constitutional norms, defining the main players in relation to the concept of national security, national interests and basic threats, were developed within a framework of National Security in 1997.

As of 2000, 'the Concept' has been updated. Following the first reading of the new version of the concept, parliament took a decision to prepare a Law 'On the Fundamentals of the National Security of Ukraine'. This was adopted in 2003. The law laid firm foundations for the functioning of the national security system of Ukraine and most importantly defined the state's priorities in terms of national interests. In particular, the Euro-Atlantic aspirations of Ukraine are set in the document.

At the same time, experience in the implementation of this law has shown that it needs to be revised. It is necessary to take into account the experience of other countries of the world, in particular the USA, whose legislation defines the system, procedures and mechanisms of actions of the state bodies in the field of national security. Threats and challenges to national security as well as key lines of state policy are defined in the National Security Strategy, which changes in accordance with the assessment of the security situation once every several years. The primary law of the USA 'On National Security' has been in force since 1947.

Changing the legislative approach to national security is a complex business. It is necessary however during the development of a new version of the Law 'On the Fundamentals of National Security of Ukraine' to define at the legislative level the system of management of national security of Ukraine. This would include the responsible actors, their functions and mechanisms of reaction to changes in the security situation, procedures for the adoption of state decisions and the implementation of responsibility. Questions of terminology and definitions could receive less attention, unlike the current legislative practice. Ultimately, the law is a not a monograph.

Finally one should have the courage to call a spade a spade. Modern euphemisms like militia (folk militia) and 'internal troops' lost their true meaning long ago. It is hoped that arguments surrounding words and terms, such as 'police', which referred to the German auxiliary police during the occupation, will not unduly influence legislators.

The proposed approach will help eliminate present contradictions between this law and the National Security Strategy as well as more clearly define their fields. At the same time, such an approach is absolutely logical in terms of constitutional powers of the head of state, who is responsible for general management in the field of national security and defence.

Another legislative problem is the weakness and insufficient formalisation of the procedures of activity of state authorities in crisis situations. The Law of Ukraine 'On the Legal Regime of a State of Emergency' regulates the actions of the state only in critical situations that require the limitation of the rights and freedoms of citizens. History shows, however, that de facto there are a number of transitional states from ordinary to extraordinary, and crises require the application of instruments necessary for specific situations.

A good example of a crisis of transitional character is the events of July 2006 in Feodosiya, when artificially instigated protests by marginal political forces cast doubt on the conduct of international military training and the capability of the Ukrainian state on the whole. The process of resolution revealed the inefficiency of the executive powers procedures in crisis situations. For this reason, clear mechanisms and procedures of state authorities in similar transitional situations are needed.

Item 7 of Article 5 of the Law of Ukraine 'On the National Security and Defence Council of Ukraine' (NSDCU) introduces the concept of 'a crisis situation which threatens national security'. In such situations, NSDCU powers are identical to its powers during martial law or a state of emergency. The necessity to define the transitional state between ordinary and extraordinary situations at the legislative level in conditions of profound societal transformations is undoubtable. The criteria for defining crisis situations that threaten national security and the mechanisms with which to tackle them are nonexistent.

There are a number of laws which regulate the activity of the security sector. These include 'On the National Security and Defence Council of Ukraine', 'On Defence of Ukraine', 'On the Security Service of Ukraine', 'On the Intelligence Services' and 'On Counter-Intelligence Service of Ukraine'. Some laws regulate separate activity areas in the field of national security. In particular, this concerns the Law 'On Defence of Ukraine'.

In January 2007, the president of Ukraine approved the 'National Security Strategy of Ukraine'. Over twelve years, NSDCU implemented more than 100 decisions. The head of state signed an enormous amount of acts which regulate certain questions, including the appointment of the leadership of military formations.

Quite a few decisions were adopted by the government in accordance with Article 116 of the constitution. According to Item 1 of this Article, the Cabinet of Ministers receives the powers in relation to the provision of state sovereignty. Item 7 states the Cabinet is responsible for carrying out measures aimed at the provision of defence capacity and national security public order, the fight against criminality, foreign economic activity and customs matters.

Currently, the main problem is not the quality of the laws which are adopted but the imperfection of mechanisms and procedures of their implementation. A low level of implementation discipline is the result. According to NSDCU estimation, '1 June 2007 was the deadline for the implementation of 433 tasks, of which, according to the current information, only 188 or 43% were executed'.[19] According to the statements of the NSDCU secretariat, the situation has barely changed since the publication of the figures.

In order to increase the effectiveness of the scheme, 'decision–implementation' within the national security systems of Ukraine has to be resolved. Every decision has to be supported by the proper financial, intellectual and other resources. Today, according to some analyses, a considerable number of NSDCU decisions remained unfulfilled because of the shortage of resources, above all of the financial ones.

The adopted state decisions and documents as a whole address a wide array of issues, however, eight basic focus areas can be identified. It is clear that ecological, social, economic and humanitarian problems are important but against this background, the problems of external and internal political and military security can be lost. This concerns the NSDCU, which from the outset had wide powers governing its activity but that have over the last years expanded in ways that are not always justifiable.

Therefore, there is a need to identify a narrow focus area and discuss the traditional security problems with which diplomats, the military, secret service agents and counter-intelligence agents have had to deal.

---

[19] Dovidka do pytannya poryadku dennoho zasidannya RNBOU vid 15.06.2007: 'Pro stan vykonannya rishen' Rady natsional'noyi bezpeky i oborony Ukrayiny', http://www.rainbow.gov.ua/news/564.html

The Security Situation around Ukraine: A General Description

At the beginning of the 21st century, radical changes took place not only in Ukraine but also in the Baltic-Black Sea-Caspian Sea region and in the world as a whole. The external security situation was relatively positive from the 1990s when Ukraine was receiving dividends from the disintegration of the socialist camp and the USSR. The events of September 11th began a symbolic fracture in the development of the security situation at the global, regional and national levels.

As mentioned in the National Security Strategy of Ukraine ratified in February 2007 by the head of state, 'a changing and contradictory external environment is characterised by the strengthening of factors which threaten strategic stability in the world'.[1]

Above all, this concerns increasing international competition and a widening of the gap in the levels of development and living standards among countries of the world. The battle for natural resources, especially energy resources and the means of supply has intensified. Coupled with this is the aggravation caused by a proliferation of weapons of mass destruction and the means of delivery. In his presentation at the Intelligence Congress in Nashville on 30 October 2008, the Director of National Intelligence of the USA, Michael McConnell, estimated an increased risk of international conflicts in the world over the next twenty-five to thirty years.

An increasing danger for Ukraine has been the escalation of 'frozen' conflicts as well as the emergence of new regional ones since the Russian-Georgian conflict in August 2008.

International terrorism is a dangerous disease and a sign of problems in the world that threaten the very future of civilisation.

International criminal syndicates engaged in the illegal trafficking of drugs, illegal migration and trade in people are active within the region. Organised crime is a threat to the national interests of Ukraine and countries of the Baltic-Black Sea-Caspian Sea region. Having said that, neither Europe nor North America is immune from this threat.

Negative mindsets have also affected the development of the security situation in Ukraine. Ensuring national unity to safeguard internal security has

---

1 Stratehiya natsional'noyi bezpeky Ukrayiny

been influenced by dangerous political speculation, both internally and externally.

Further, the mechanisms for adopting and implementing state decisions are poor and inefficient as a result of ongoing political instability, corruption and the incompetence of the state administration. The situation has been further exacerbated by the questionable relationship between business people and politicians. According to Transparency International, Ukraine occupies the 118th place out of 180 in terms of the level of corruption.

Threats to the economic, ecological and social security of Ukraine have substantially increased as a result of the world economic crisis and are at a precarious level. There is an urgency to deal with these problems, however, potentially effective counteraction is limited as a result of the gradual decline in relations between NATO and Russia. The fear that Ukraine will somehow become the 'grey' area between the European and Eurasian geopolitical groups (NATO) and the Collective Security Treaty Organisation (CSTO) with its opposite system of values and strategies is becoming more real.

It is within this context that the future of Ukraine rests, specifically in the development of relations and its positioning in relation to the US-Russian Federation and the EU triangle.

The relations between the USA and Russia, which had been the central focus of international policy for about half a century, gradually took a back seat on the world stage.

Notwithstanding what is said in Moscow and Kyiv, this therefore is not about basic issues of modern international relations. Relations of late among the three arms of this strategic body could not be called straightforward. The USA and EU are strategic allies, having been united by transatlantic solidarity for more than half a century. At one time, the basic task of NATO was approximately as follows: 'control Germany, keep the USA in Europe and Russia outside Europe'. The alliance executed this task skilfully.

After the collapse of the USSR and the liberation of the European Union from the Soviet threat, it was natural that some powerful forces came forward in support of complete or partial emancipation from the USA on questions of foreign policy and security. This effort was led by Berlin and represented by Schroeder with Chirac representing Fronde Paris. The peak of disagreement came in 2003 when Germany and France, as well as a few other 'old European' states, did not support the American invasion of Iraq. Predictably, the mass media and commentators made the most of the contradictions,[2] as well as the insurmountable differences between the EU and USA.

Indeed, the division of Europe emerged with an 'old' Europe, more independent in its policy and thus more inclined to listen to the Kremlin on the

---

2 Kagan R., O raye y sile. Amerika i Yevropa v novom mirovom poryadke., Moscow, 2004 [Paradise and Power: America and Europe in the New World Order].

one hand and a 'new' openly pro-American Europe, joined for known reasons by Great Britain, a country tied by special relations to the USA, on the other.

Notwithstanding Russian efforts to play an imperial game of 'divide and rule' leaders of European states, on the whole, clearly understood their potential weakness and appreciated the futility of breaking up the 'American marriage'. This realisation was made all the more acute in a world with changing geopolitical conditions and positions in the global West as well as the rapid emergence of new centres of power in South-East Asia and Latin America. The beginning of global change and the emergence of a new world order had begun.

This all became quite evident during the most critical financial-economic crisis of the last decade. Whilst the hub of this crisis was the USA, its impact was very visible in Europe.

The G20 countries whose combined Gross Domestic Product exceeds three quarters of the world economy confirmed this during the Washington summit of 14–15 November 2008. The necessity to bring an end to meetings in the G8 format and to include new participants, mainly developing countries, in the strategic management, was also discussed in Washington. Conversations about the development of the mechanisms for global governance were interesting new developments. This theme however is beyond our work and requires separate and meticulous research.

The impact of this crisis saw a change of leadership in Germany and France between 2005 and 2007 and the coming to power of more pro-Atlantic politicians of a new generation, Angela Merkel and Nicolas Sarkozy respectively. Whilst we cannot comment on the consensus of their positions, a common line is gradually being formed.

The USA, for its part, aims to strengthen this partnership. It spends money on it and even in a pre-election year adopted an unpopular decision, risking the support of the electorate for the sake of national interests. It is a good example for our politicians. In March 2008, the Pentagon adopted a decision to purchase, over the next ten to fifteen years, 179 aerial refuelling tankers for approximately US$35 billion from the European consortium EADS. Boeing, the American corporation that had supplied the US air force with aerial refuellers for almost fifty years, suddenly found itself competing with Europeans, who had concluded deals with the American corporation Northrop Grumman.

In the current US Air Force, there are 590 air tankers created mainly along the lines of a Boeing 707. Their average service life is forty-five years. The Pentagon plans to replace and downsize the entire fleet over the next thirty years. The planned budget is between US$100–200 billion.

However it is not possible to discuss the revival of a transatlantic idyll. European countries, unlike the USA, are far more interested in cordial relationships with Russia. This accounts for their significant attentiveness to their large eastern neighbour. Perhaps dependence on energy supplies from the east account for something too. Furthermore, a longer tradition of association with Russia dating from the Russian empire to the 'red' and then modern Kremlin also plays an important role.

The last dazzling manifestation of transatlantic contradictions was the compromise reached in relation to Ukraine and Georgia at the Bucharest summit of NATO in April 2008. It is a compromise and indeed a positive and acceptable outcome for Ukraine. In fact, this was the first NATO decision at the highest levels that proclaimed the inevitability of Kyiv's entry into the alliance. At the same time, Ukraine was also reminded that its future would not be decided in the White House, the Kremlin, the Champs-Elysées or even Kyiv but in Donets'k, L'viv, Vinnytsya and far beyond to the smallest village.

The Bucharest summit confirmed the democratic character of the mechanisms of political decision making by the alliance. Notwithstanding the USA's clout as the largest NATO member and the first world power, European countries had insisted on a compromise that was acceptable to them.

As a result of the establishment of the European Union as an independent geopolitical player (whose wheels have slowed down recently on account of the problems with the union's constitutional arrangements), there has been a tendency toward gradual emancipation of Russia-EU relations from influence by the USA on the whole. Unlike economic processes, this political process did not take an easily definable format. Despite the disagreement of Poland and Lithuania, the renewal of EU-Russia negotiations in November 2008 in relation to the development of a new general agreement is evidence of a gradual formation of separate political relations or possibly even a hint of 'Schröderisation' (Nemtsov, B) in the European Union. It should be noted that 'Schröderisation' is not about the construction of an EU-Russia union so much as the gentle softening of Washington's attitude towards the Kremlin and development of Russia's own domestic policy towards the West of deeper involvement with it.

The fact is that Europe's policy towards Russia will for some time continue to follow that of Washington where a détente seems certain—relationships between the USA and Russia have been somewhat difficult since the end of the Cold War.

Relations between the two have been transformed from the unequal partnership that existed during the early period of Yeltsin's presidency (personified in A. Kozirev who was the first minister for foreign affairs of the Russian Federation) through a gradual cooling and even through several crises. The latter was symbolised by his successor, Yevgeny Primakov, turning around over the Atlantic Ocean en route to a meeting in the United States. This related to hard competition over geopolitical positions and issues in Eurasia, which now, according to D. Medvedev, are regarded within the Kremlin as containing exclusive areas of interest for the Russian Federation.

At the same time, the fact that the Russian leadership perceives relations with the USA as a zero sum game remains unchanged. The perception amongst Russians is that the United States remains the main opponent of the Russian Federation. Thus, in the opinion of many Russian leaders and experts, Washington takes all possible measures to ensure the destruction of Russia.

At the beginning of the C20, upon the termination of the period of active reforms of the 1990s and the establishment of relative stability, Moscow engaged in a substantial rethinking of its role in the world. In particular, it abandoned its global claims, closed its military bases in Lourdes (Cuba) and Kamran (Vietnam) and embraced a strategy aimed at transforming Russia into an energy superpower and regional leader in North Eurasia.[3]

This vision is reflected in the key strategic documents acknowledged during V. Putin's first term in office. It includes the National Security Concept (presidential decree of 10 January 2000), the Foreign Policy Concept (presidential decree of 28 June 2000) and the Energy Strategy for the period until 2020 ratified by the government on 28 August 2003.

In appearances and statements in 2003–2007, V. Putin elaborated these views and formulated a vision of the future world order. According to him, an international system in which the economic and security spheres of America, Europe, Russia and the Far East will cooperate on the basis of shared principles will come into being. To the contrary, a number of American experts, most important among them being Zbigniew Brzezinski and Samuel Huntington, see the future of Russia as a country incorporated into the European part of the world led by the USA. The leadership of the Russian Federation hoped for convergence of the post-Soviet space led by Russia with the civilised north as one of its majority shareholders, with a principled simultaneous preservation of the authoritarian regime. V. Putin noted: 'We fully realise what Russia is, its place in the world and our possibilities. But Russia, with all its misfortunes, is a country with traditions and national interests. It is a country which will never serve somebody else's foreign-policy interests'. This is probably exactly the model personified by A. Chubais in the expressive slogan, 'We want liberal empire!'

In 2007, some changes in this approach occurred. The Kremlin now wishes to see the world as a system of different independent civilisations, each of which has its own values, norms and rules. This view denies the presence of values and ideas common to all mankind and thus permanently ruins the ideological base of modern international relations.

---

3 In August 2008, after the visit of the Russian officials I. Sechin and V. Patrushev to Havana, signs of Russian return in the Western hemisphere appeared, however, it is too early to examine these attempts seriously.

Similar ideas were more clearly expressed in an updated version of the Foreign Policy Concept of the Russian Federation (hereinafter the Concept) approved on 12 July in 2008 by the President of the Russian Federation Dmitri Medvedev. The document outlined the succession of foreign policy of the Russian Federation. It develops the stipulations of the previous version of the Concept of 28 June 2000. The previous structure was almost entirely retained. In accordance with the preferences of the new master of the Kremlin, quite a declarative priority of foreign policy was added: 'Supremacy of law in international relations'. Because of considerable additions, the size of the document almost doubled.

The Concept reflects a traditional Russian perception of the country as the fortress in a state of siege which expects a hostile assault day after day. In fact, this model as that of the 'Third Rome' is an Orthodox-Byzantine perception of Holy Rus'—a unique orthodox kingdom surrounded by the enemies of veritable faith.

The authors of the Concept were considerably influenced by the ideas of O. Spengler, A. Toynbee and Russian Eurasian scholars, in particular L. Gumilev. In the 2008 version, words deriving from the concept 'civilisation' were mentioned thirteen times (in 2000 not a single time). This indicates a substantial transformation—the civilisation theory and idea of separateness and uniqueness of the Russian civilisation, the 'Russian World', became the ideological basis of Russian foreign policy.

The tone has fundamentally changed: from careful to extraordinarily offensive. For example, in the 2000 Concept the adjective 'certain' is used twice, while in 2008 this word is not used at all. The Russian Federation saw a political and economic upturn and hoped to get all possible dividends from the existing situation. The grumblings about the concept, advocated by Putin, for the 'strengthening of tendencies towards the formation of a one-polar world with power and economic domination by the USA' were replaced by the architects of Medvedev's foreign policy. They proclaimed 'the loss by the historical West of monopoly over globalisation processes…' a modern version of 'the decline of Europe'. The document on the whole is a vivid example of revanchist ideology.

No less important for Ukraine is the change of approach in relations with the Commonwealth of Independent States (CIS). An accent on integration and national security has been substantially weakened. The successive introduction of market principles in trade-economic relations and the preservation of 'cultural-civilisational heritage', and above all the advancement of the Russian culture and language guaranteeing the rights for Russian minorities, are the factors that have contributed to this weakening.

For the first time the Concept directly mentioned Ukraine: 'Russia preserves a negative attitude toward the expansion of NATO, in particular membership of Ukraine and Georgia in the Alliance'.

There are other innovations, for example with regard to relations with the USA (culture of management of differences and the economic basis of relations), with the EU (strengthening of the union and its ability to achieve shared positions), with China (proclamation of strategic partnership and emphasis on the role of the Shanghai Cooperation Organisation).

Finally, in complete accordance with the existing two-centre power in Russia, a sentence was added at the end of the text that the government of the Russian Federation plays a role in foreign policy of the country.

Further prospects of such a course for Russia, are at odds with the Concept given events in Georgia in August 2008. Strengthening of authoritarian tendencies in the world, evidenced by some of the public processes in the USA, create quite favourable conditions for the attempts by the Russian Federation leadership to continue its sturdy course. However, from the very beginning this strategy conflicted with the interests of western countries created by their political elite educated during the Cold War years. It is this and not democratic values which ultimately determine the negative reactions to the Kremlin by the USA and to a certain extent the EU countries.

In a speech by V. Putin at the Munich Security Conference on 10 February 2007,[4] a new approach to international relations was declared for the first time. A game aimed at the deterioration of relations in 2007 was for many reasons advantageous for the Kremlin. Above all, the revival of an image of the enemy as represented by the USA and its allies was instrumental in mobilising the support of the electorate prior to the presidential elections. The winning conditions were set by the first actions of the future president. These were perceived as 'détente'.

At the same time, many Americans welcomed the return of the ghost of the eastern threat, which enabled them not to have to develop new approaches but take advantage of the already tested and reliable old ones.

Barack Obama based his election campaign on the spread of democracy on the principles of the National Security Strategy of the USA: 'the USA will use the possibility for the spread of advantages of freedom all over the world. We will work actively to bring the hope of democracy, development, free market and trade in every corner of the world'.[5]

Even more so, according to the American magazine *The Nation*, the leading foreign-policy advisers to Obama are Michael McFaul and Zbigniew

---

4 Vystupleniye V.V., Putina, 10.02.2007, http://www.v-v-putin.ru/munhen10–02–2007.html

5 National Security Strategy of the USA, 2002, p. 4.

Brzezinski,[6] known for their tough stance on Russia, and his secretary of state is Hillary Clinton.

In a speech given in February 2008 and eloquently titled 'Democratic Imperative', D. Miliband, Britain's Minister of Foreign Affairs, also illustrated this traditional attitude. He noted that 'the West must, as before, help in the spread of democracy in the modern world including in a military way'. The spread of the 'Western model' must be 'the most promising project'. 'Deep concern' about errors, in particular in Iraq and Afghanistan, should not hinder this.[7]

The USA and Great Britain do not limit themselves to tough statements. Consistent US policy aimed at the deployment of anti-missile defence, granting of political refuge by London to the opponents of the Russian regime, the last case being that of O. Tregubova, 'the Kremlin digger', and its tough stance on espionage—the latter influenced by the Federal Security Service of the Russian Federation, in particular in relation to the company TNKBP and the representative office of the British Council in the Russian Federation.

The relations between the USA and Russia deteriorated substantially on the eve of the Russian presidential elections in March 2008, the first occurring after the disintegration of the USSR. Large-scale manoeuvres by the Russian naval and air forces in the Bay of Biscay in the Atlantic Ocean in which the flagship of the Russian fleet, the heavy aircraft carrier *Admiral Kuznetsov* participated, took place at that time. On 22 January 2008 during these manoeuvres, the British air force used fighters to accompany the Russian Tu-160 strategic bombers, which came very close to the borders of Britain's air space. The Russian Federation also interrupted its participation in the Treaty on Conventional Armed Forces in Europe (CFE).

On 5 February 2008, the Director of National Intelligence of the USA Michael McConnell, noted in Washington during the hearings in the Senate Committee on Secret Services that the USA is afraid that Russia, China and other oil-extracting countries and members of OPEC, can use their increasing financial potential for achievement of global political aims. This idea is hardly novel and illustrates well the changeability of political orientations: almost a century ago, after the end of the First World War, no American politician doubted that the financial power of the United States was what precisely determined its leading geopolitical mission.

According to estimates based on oil profits, Russia aims to establish control over energy supplies and transportation networks in Europe and East

---

6 Robert Dreyfuss, 'The Rise and McFaul of Obama's Russian Policy', 07/02/2008, http://www.thenation.com/blogs/dreyfuss/334120

7 Wintour, Patrick, 'Miliband: UK has moral duty to intervene', http://www.guardian.co.uk/politics/2008/feb/12/foreignpolicy.iraq

Asia. The Russian Armed Forces also began to recover from a protracted decline.

China, on the contrary, aims to gain access to global markets, resources and technology for its growing economy. It aims to establish constructive mutual relations with the USA and other countries. As its influence grows, Beijing hopes for greater respect for its interests by other countries.

Active intelligence activity of the Russian special services resumed in the European Union and the USA. According to the same estimations, Russia and China have access to the American computer networks for collection of intelligence data, however, there is a concern that they can also aspire to weaken or eliminate the information infrastructure.

It is significant that the offensive by the Russian special services is carried out not only against the USA but also the EU countries, including friendly Germany. In particular, the Federal Office for the Protection of the Constitution (BFV—counter-intelligence of the Federal Republic of Germany), in the annual report for 2007, notes that 'foreign spies who obtain information about hi-tech production in an illegal way pose an increasing threat to the German business'. Thus special danger is posed by the actions of the Russian SVR – Foreign Intelligence Service.

Unlike the People's Republic of China, which focuses on espionage via the internet, the Russian Federation uses traditional methods—secret agents and other persons for access to information in an illegal way. Students, experts and interns from many countries actively collect business information in Germany, according to the BFV report.

According to German counter-intelligence officers, the situation is complicated by the fact that the government of the Federal Republic of Germany is usually reserved when the matter concerns China and the Russian Federation: Berlin aspires to rapprochement with Moscow and Beijing.

The activity of Russian secret service agents was disclosed in Great Britain, Latvia, Estonia and other European countries between 2007 and 2008.

At the same time, Russian authorities attempted to build the mechanisms of mutually beneficial relations with the USA. The speech by the First Vice Premier Minister of the Russian Federation S. Ivanov at the Munich conference *On Security Policy* on 10 February 2008, is a good illustration. It was in stark contrast with the speech by V. Putin during the meeting of the State Council of the Russian Federation on 8 February, in which he discussed the race of armaments and a multi-polar world. S. Ivanov was quite moderate and careful. It is notable that these conciliatory statements were made after the proclamation of independence by Kosovo.

By April, steps directed at the improvement of relations were being taken. After a compromise by NATO, supported by the Kremlin, at the Bucharest summit, on 6 April 2008 negotiations between the US president and the Russian Federation took place in Sochi (Russia). As a result of this, an American-Russian Declaration on the strategic framework was adopted. According to V. Putin, the document did not resolve all problems but it summarised the achievements of the two presidents during eight years as heads of state.

The British press noted that George Bush did not succeed in resolving the key question related to reaching an agreement on an anti-missile defence system and opening new doors on relations. However, D. Medvedev and B. Obama inherited a well-referenced list of old and difficult problems as well as histories of constructive relations at the level of head of state.

Efforts of the Kremlin became even more peaceful after the transfer of power from V. Putin to the newly elected President of the Russian Federation D. Medvedev. During the G8 meeting in July 2008, Medvedev presented proposals concerning the improvement of the global security framework. In particular, he suggested the signing of a European pact of security, creating a new system of security in Europe replacing NATO, the OSCE and the CSTO. According to *The International Herald Tribune* 'the proposal is not so much about the improvement of the international climate as about the continuation of an old soviet tradition of advancement by peaceful initiatives directed at the destruction of the unity of international groups'.[8]

The Russian-Georgian conflict substantially complicated the situation but did not halt the re-establishment of the system of relations between the Russian Federation, the USA and the EU countries. The revision of the situation by western investors in the Russian Federation was a direct economic impact, reinforced by the matter of the company Mechel.[9] In conditions of the world economic crisis, the situation resulted in a swift falling of the stock market and strengthening of isolationist, anti-western and above all anti-American sentiments in Russian society.

Independent analysts can learn two basic lessons from the Caucasian events. First, the leadership of the Russian Federation is ready to revive its dominance on the territory of the former Soviet Union with all possible means, including with the use of military force.

Second, the USA and the EU do not presently possess the necessary capacity to make the realisation of the Kremlin strategy on quashing the rebellious countries on the territory of the former USSR impossible.

For this reason, in a political-diplomatic way, a diplomatic *sur place* between the Russian Federation and the West, above all the EU countries, became the result of the conflict for the restoration of damaged communications.

---

8 Dempsey, Judy, The International Herald Tribune, 28.07.08.

9 Gurvich V., Institutsional'nye faktory ekonomicheskogo krizisa, http://polit.ru/lectures/2008/10/28/krisis.html

Rhetoric became harsher at the propagandist front. An insightful reflection of the mood of the Russian foreign policy establishment was the reaction of Moscow to another hard statement by republican presidential candidate J. McCain. On 29 July 2008, an unknown Russian diplomat declared that Russia could allow itself to have no relationships with partners if they so desired. No need to mention the information campaign around the August 2008 events in the Caucasus.

The Kremlin continued to unite allies against the USA. Evidence of this is the July 2008 visit of the President of Venezuela Hugo Chavez to Moscow and the September training of the strategic aviation and fleet of the Russian Federation within the territory of this Latin American country.

In an address by President Medvedev on 5 November 2008, two hours after Barack Obama was elected president of the USA, Medvedev announced that Russia would deploy *Iskander* missile systems in the Kaliningrad region in case of the need for deployment, if necessary, against the anti-ballistic missile defence in Europe. This should be understood as sheer propaganda given the true military meaning of 'asymmetric response' and the absence of mass-produced *Iskanders* in the Russian Federation.

A series of steps aimed at softening relations was the reason behind President Medvedev's appearance at the international conference on *Questions of Foreign Policy* in Evian (France) on 8 October 2008. Along with its classical anti-American appeal, the tone of Medvedev's speech was significantly gentler even by comparison with the Foreign Policy Concept of the Russian Federation. It focused on military issues, accentuating the need to abandon lines of division in Europe and to rebuild more effective security mechanisms.

One angle taken in a dialogue on the creation of mechanisms of cooperation, attempts to resolve urgent problems between the Kremlin and the White House, at the expense of other countries, above all of Ukraine. Evidence of that is a position expressed by Henry Kissinger at the beginning of July 2008.[10] The patriarch of American foreign policy calls to give up the membership of Ukraine in NATO on condition of providing real independence of Kyiv. Such an idea is explained by an unwillingness to unnecessarily irritate the Kremlin.

Similar views are not prevalent in the current American establishment. The US ambassador to Ukraine, William Taylor, noted on 23 April 2008 at an international conference in Kyiv that support for Ukraine's membership in NATO is a constant aim of Washington's foreign policy, regardless of who the master of the White House was over the next four years. Taylor repeated this

10 Kissinger H., 'The Unconventional Wisdom about Russia', Tribune Media Services, June 30, 2008 http://www.henryakissinger.com/arti cles/tms063008.html

position in a statement issued after the election of Barack Obama as president of the USA.

The Deputy Secretary of State for Europe and Eurasia David Merkel stressed on 25 July 2008 that the United States did not plan to stop supporting Kyiv, notwithstanding the political instability. He is also convinced that the appeals of the former U.S. Secretary of State Henry Kissinger about not interfering in the sphere of interests of Russia and preventing Ukraine from moving closer to NATO membership cannot find 'understanding' in the American administration. 'If one believes that it is necessary to give to Russia the sphere of its interests and not to develop relationships with its neighbours as it annoys Russia, then Moscow will know that it has an influence lever. Then the sphere of its interests will simply begin to widen. At the same time, the field of our negotiations with Russia will narrow', observed the representative of the State Department. Once again, the US Congress supported membership of Ukraine in NATO in a resolution.

At the same time, a scenario of Ukraine moving into the 'grey area' as a result of exchanges between the USA and the Russian Federation should not be eliminated from the list of credible scenarios. At a time when there is a radical rethinking of the foreign policy of the George Bush Jr. administration, preventing this scenario must become a matter of priority in Ukrainian strategy.

This task acquires special importance when competition between the community of democratic countries and successful autocracies (China and Russia) is accelerating. For the first time in twenty years, Russia questioned a liberal-democratic model of social development, making futile the hopes of 'the end of history', as put by Francis Fukuyama. Therefore, a new period of the 'Big Game' began and it is the responsibility of the national elite to effectively play by the rules.

The Ukrainian Power Elite in the Light of National Security

In modern political thought, there are a great number of approaches to determine the key factors required for internal change. In the Ukrainian situation, the problem is the Ukrainian establishment or elite. It is a historical fact dating back to Plato and Aristotle. In more contemporary times it is the works of Vilfredo Pareto and Gaetano Mosca. They all posit that the manner in which the elite execute its functions is the way that the state functions. The fact that the Ukrainian establishment is incapable of carrying out society-wide functions became a topic for public discussion long ago. However, its claims have no bounds, with the proclamation of itself as the 'new Ukrainian aristocracy'.

The elite defines a group of people who understand the national interests of the country, its political, economic, geographical position and who influence the creation of internal and foreign policy as well as its implementation.

Undoubtedly such people should be highly educated, trained in an all-round way with flexible thinking and, most importantly, with a heightened sense of responsibility about the country's future. The elite must sense the challenges of history, be able to react to them and find adequate solutions. Finally these people must think not only for the day but more importantly the future.

Below are the results of studies on quantitative descriptions of the modern Ukrainian elite.

Studies conducted between 2002 and 2005 by the National Institute of Strategic Studies, however, were not released in time.[1] Notwithstanding the fact that the prepared materials are somewhat outdated, they remain sufficiently relevant for the current situation.[2] It is notable that the Orange Revolution did not result in the renewal of elites but rather their reshuffling.

---

1 Lytvynenko O.V., Palamarchuk V.M., Yanishevs'kyy S.O., Konakh V.K., Palamarchuk M.O., Sakharenko O.V., Matushans'ka N.V., Chapter 4, Ukrayins'ki elity pered Maydanom: stan i tendentsiyi rozvytku, Suspil'nopolitychna model' Ukrayiny. Personal archive of O. Lytvynenko.

2 We should note that a series of reference books 'Who is who in Ukraine' (published by the Petro Mohyla Kyiv Scientific Society and the publishing house 'K.I.S.') is the most useful integrated source of research on the modern Ukrainian elite. It is possible to consider the circle of persons included in the edition in a certain way the most representative representation of

Throughout years of independence, there was an enormous deficit of the real elite. What was the cause of this situation? The answer relates not solely to morality and various other problems faced by society but also of the global situation and the specific hallmarks of the origins of the Ukrainian establishment.

Very important are the observations of Giovanni Arrighi,[3] who in the known study on 'The Long Twentieth Century' refers to an example of the Italian elite of the Renaissance period. The latter invested in neither production nor trade expeditions nor the creation or recreation of capital but in treasures. This conduct may be explained by the general economic situation, in particular by the characteristics of the world division of labour and the system of political risks at that time.

Presently, as in the Renaissance period in Italy, the situation forces the Ukrainian elite to accumulate treasures and liquid assets, which contributes in the same way to the problem of the establishment's values, its so called non-ideological attitude, pragmatism and general low culture.

Who belongs to the Ukrainian establishment presently? Without particularly thinking about responsibility vis-à-vis history and the Ukrainian people, almost all deputies of the Verkhovna Rada of independent Ukraine of all convocations consider themselves overtly 'elite'. Endless 'changes of guard' in Cabinet (whose members sometimes do not have time to take up their positions) resulted in a more cautious attitude by government officials in referencing them as elite. Certain representatives of big business, practically all stars of show business and pop culture and sometimes sport as well as politically active groups of people such as TV political scientists consider themselves elites.
The basic general features of this diverse group are:

- Achieved financial well-being and money, accumulating more money being their primary purpose;

---

elites (the establishment) in contemporary Ukraine. (Belonging to the elite is determined on the basis of a formal characteristic, i.e. the occupation of a certain place in a particular hierarchy in a given sphere of public life. In this context, the terms 'elite' and 'establishment' are used interchangeably). The attempt of publishers of the reference book to include the most significant persons in different spheres of public life (the 2004 edition referenced below includes data on 7,234 persons) makes it the most useful and adequate source for studies on structural features of elite. It should be noted that the present quantitative analysis is not an exhaustive description of the modern Ukrainian elite, however, it helps to identify a number of tendencies characteristic of the leading class of our society. It should also be noted that the results of the second stage of research are presented in this chapter. The first stage was carried out in 2002, which analysed the materials for 2001.

3 Arrighi, Giovanni, Dolgiy dvadtsatyy vek. Den'gi, vlast' i istoki nashego vremeni, Moscow: Territoriya budushego, 2006, pp. 142–156. [The Long Twentieth Century: Money, Power, and the Origins of Our Times].

- Aspiration to use money to enter into politics in order to convert this entry into power;
- Absolute misunderstanding and aggressive non-acceptance of freedom, justice and national interests.

Among persons included in the reference book '*Who is Who in Ukraine. 2004*', representatives of local self-government bodies constitute 14.6%, civil servants 29.0%, and politicians 7.7%. The share of business representatives was 0.5% with leaders of enterprise at 5.5% (see Diagram 1). If the data of 2004 is compared with that of 2001, no significant changes occurred.

The Ukrainian elite is currently composed of people who at the beginning of the 1990s were able to either legalise shadow capital or convert such capital into power and connections, or to take part in 'grey' or 'dark' money laundering. Often it is a combination of all three types. Powerlessness and the absence of a counter-elite (exterminated in seventy years of communist rule in what was Soviet Ukraine) and the consequent involvement of only Soviet forces in the new establishment played a crucial role. Even Soviet dissidents (in no way is the intention to diminish their enormous merits and genuine courage) were part of Soviet society. What is clear, however, is that these conditions have enabled the group of asset owners who have negatively impacted on the productive character of capital.

Diagram 1: Occupations

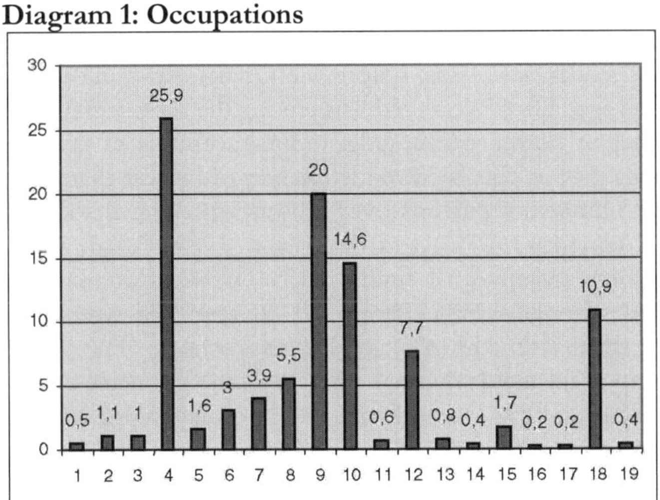

Conventional signs:
1 – workers of the bank sphere; 2 – military; 3 – civil society leaders; 4 – civil servants; 5 – diplomats; 6 – artists; 7 – workers of the mass media; 8 – leaders of enterprises, business school; 9 – scholars; 10 – civil servants of local self-

government bodies; 11 – employees of tax authorities; 12 – politicians; 13 – law enforcement officials; 14 – trade unions; 15 – religious leaders; 16 – employees of SSU; 17 – sportsmen; 18 – judges; 19 – representatives of foundations.

These theories confirm the data of quantitative analysis. A meaningful quality of the elite is a person with quite a high level of heredity, namely with connections to the elite of both modern and Soviet Ukraine times, with the basic origins as the present elite. The data confirms that 18.1% of representatives of the modern elite worked for state authorities at different levels during Soviet times (until 1991), 29.3% in the scientific field, 10.1% in Komsomol and party organs and 0.6% in the organs of the KGB. These numbers greatly differentiate the Ukrainian establishment from the Russian one.

Interestingly, participants of dissident movements accounted for only 0.8% and workers 0.6% (see Diagram 2). This data is practically identical to the materials for 2001. Thus it is possible to come to the conclusion about the evolutionary character of the elite in independent Ukraine during the time of Kravchuk and Kuchma and the insignificant influence of representatives of the counter-elite of the Soviet era.

The next area of analysis is the generational structure of the elite (Diagram 3). Every generation of elite has its particular features and character predefined by the specificities of the time of its emergence and socialisation and, in particular, its diverse predisposition for change.

More detailed analyses of generational structure divided by types of activity illustrates differences from the general type, though simultaneously represents general tendencies. Thus, before the Orange Revolution the largest number of persons aged 50–60 years old was among the representatives of local and regional bodies of power (56%), judges (56%), officials of tax authorities (5%) and diplomats (54%). This is currently the area of biggest change.

The largest number of persons over 60 was among civil society leaders (38%), leaders of enterprise (27%) and diplomats (27%). People 30–40 years old were among representatives of funds – 13%, workers of trade unions – 11% and business schools – 11%. People 20–30 years old were among the representatives of the mass media (4%) and business schools (4%).

Another important factor that has influenced the character of the elite is its mainly rural origin—51.9%. Accordingly, 34.7% of elite representatives were born in towns and town-type villages, and 13.4% in cities with more than a million inhabitants (see Diagram 4).

Although these numbers do not correspond to the current all-Ukrainian situation, they are representative of the processes that took place between thirty and fifty years previous. Today in Ukraine 32. 8% of the population lives in rural areas and 67.2% in cities. These processes greatly defined the social-psychological make up of the modern elite.

Diagram 2: Type of activity in the Ukrainian SSR

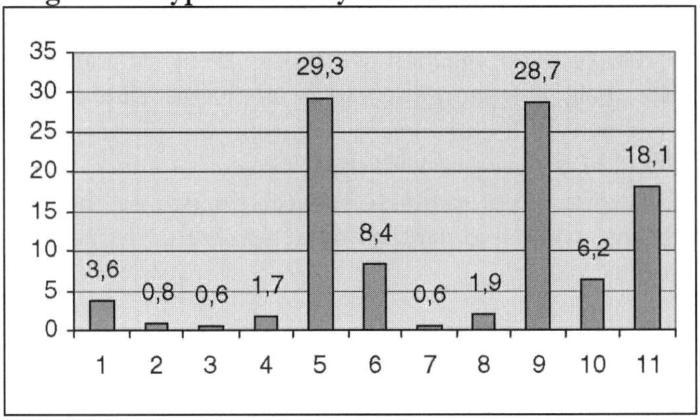

Conventional signs:
1 – servicemen; 2 – dissidents; 3 – workers of KGB; 4 – Komsomol organs; 5 – scholars; 6 – party organs; 7 – workers; 8 – priests; 9 – officials; 10 – creative intelligentsia; 11 – economy management

Diagram 3: Age (in %)

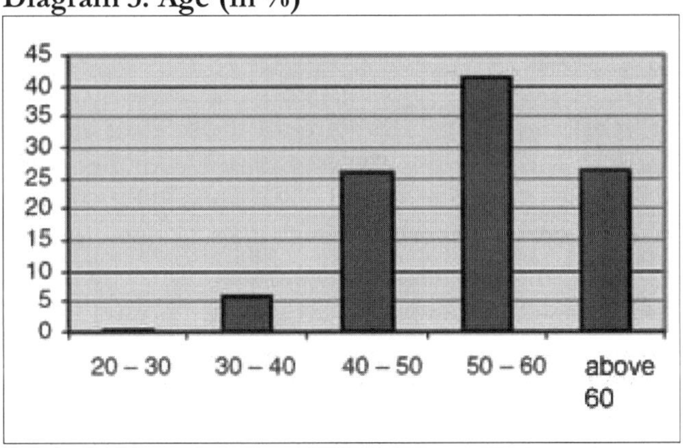

Concerning the place of birth of representatives of the new Ukrainian elite, 12% were born outside Ukraine in the Russian Federation and 1.6% in other republics of the USSR. 1.1% of persons were born outside the Soviet Union. Thus, 85.3% of elite representatives were born in Ukraine. The majority of them were born in Kyiv and the Kyiv region—16% (10% and 6%, respectively). Second place is occupied by the Donets'k region with 7% and third place by Vinnytsya with 6%. In Dnipropetrovs'k, L'viv, Poltava and Kharkiv regions, 5% respectively were born there. The smallest number of representatives of the elite was born in the Chernivtsi region (1%). In Zakarpattya, Mykolaiv, Kherson and Chernihiv regions, as well as in the

Autonomous Republic of Crimea, 2% respectively were born. Although in general this represents a nationwide distribution of population, there is a certain disparity: Ten percent of the population lives in the Donets'k region whilst the percentage of elite there constitutes seven. In Kyiv, the elite constitute ten percent of an area in which only five percent of the population lives. In Zhytomyr, the situation is the same with three percent of elite in a population of five percent. However, the proportions between the two are the same in the Poltava and L'viv regions at five percent, three percent in Ternopil' and two percent in Kherson.

Diagram 4: Origin

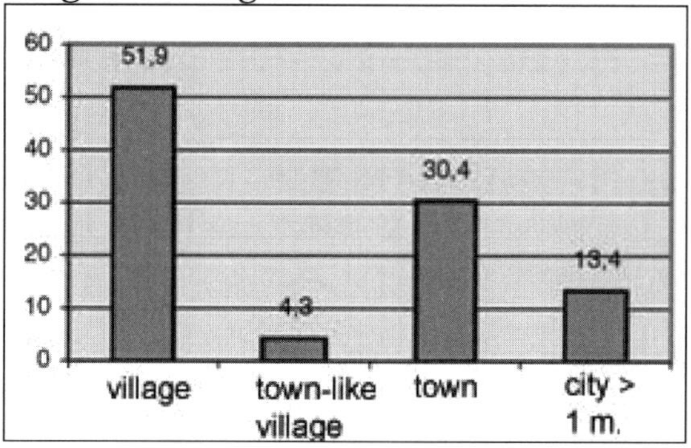

An important factor in distinguishing the features of the modern elite is its high level of formal education. The most popular are humanities and education 37.9 (39.5%), technical training 34 (35.5%) and economics 11.2 (10.6%). The smallest number of elite representatives received musical training 0.5 (0.7%), religious education 1.7 (21%) and military education 2.7 (3.6%). There are only 0.3 (0.6%) persons with secondary or special secondary education (see Diagram 5). Thus in comparison with 2001, there is a slow but gradual departure of the establishment from the Soviet legacy in education. While the share of graduates from engineering and higher military educational establishments is greatly diminished, the number of economists and lawyers increased. These trends continue.

It is even more interesting that 31.8 (31.6%) of persons in the study have a degree. Among them, 34.1 (47.5%) have a degree of candidates of sciences, 27.2 (30.4%) doctors of sciences, 22.4 (8.9%) members of the Academy of Sciences and 14.8 (12.5%) academics (see Diagram 6).

Among candidates and doctors of sciences, most persons are between 50–60 years old, 43% and 42% respectively.

In relation to areas of specialisation, the majority of persons are specialised in economics 17.7 (22.7%), in the technical sphere 19 (20.3%), in law 10.2 (12.8%), in geography 0.5 (0.2%) and in sociology 0.5%. The share of degrees increased in the field of state administration from 0.3% in 2001 to 1.5% in 2004.

Only 0.9 (2.4%) of elite representatives were educated or interned abroad, of those 0.3 (1.6%) in the USA or Canada. 10.4% of representatives of the establishment studied in Russia and other CIS countries in 2004 (see Diagram 8).

The data on the higher educational establishments from which elites graduated is also interesting. According to the reference book '*Who is Who in Ukraine*', the Kyiv National Taras Shevchenko University occupies first place (16.6 %), with the Kharkiv National Yaroslav Mudryy Legal Academy in second place (7.6%) and in third place the Lviv National Ivan Franko University (4.7%).

Diagram 5: Education

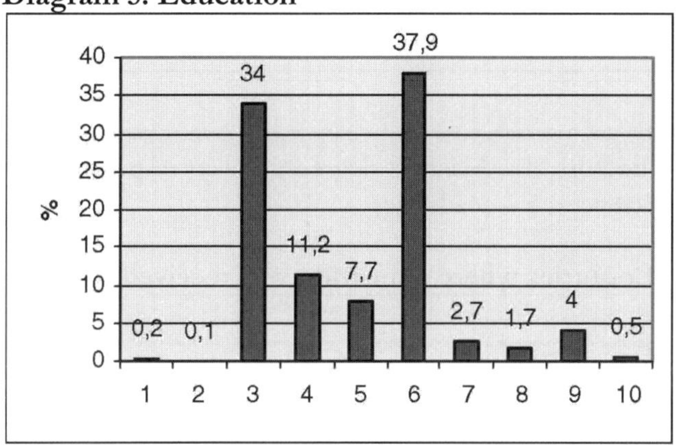

Conventional signs:
1 – secondary; 2 –special secondary; 3 – technical; 4 – economics; 5 – natural sciences; 6 – humanities; 7 – military; 8 – religious; 9 – medical; 10 – musical

Diagram 6: Degrees (in %)

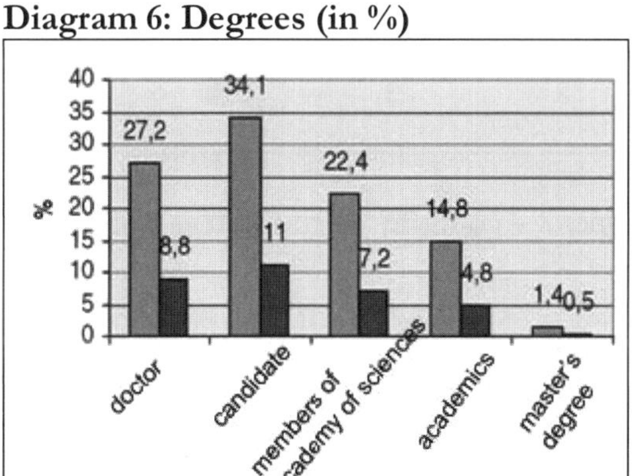

Diagram 7: Degrees according to age (in %)

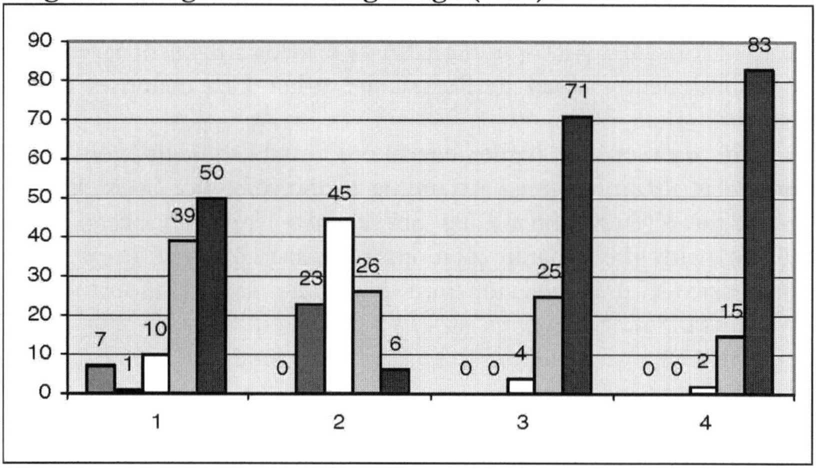

Conventional signs:
1 – candidates; 2 – doctors; 3 – Master's degrees; 4 – corresponding members of the Academy of Sciences; 5 – academics

Diagram 8: Countries where education was received (in %)

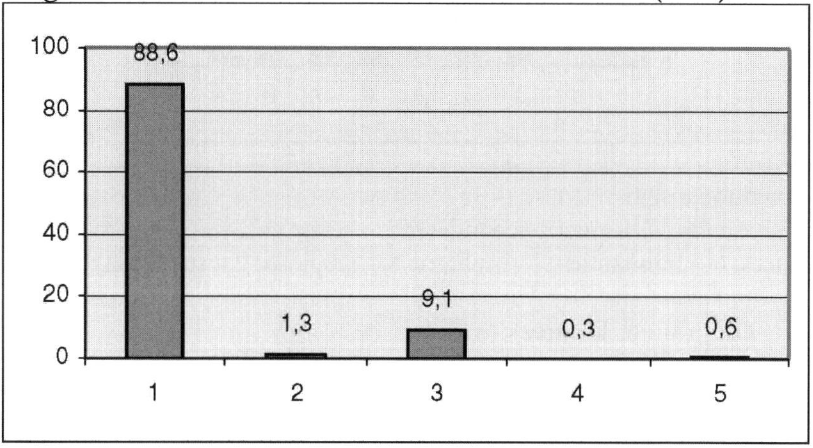

Conventional signs: 1 – Ukraine; 2 – countries of the former USSR; 3 – Russia; 4 – USA; 5 – other countries

The national composition of the modern elite is as follows: 80.2% are Ukrainians, 14.4% are Russians, 1.4 % Jews, 0.7% Byelorussians and 0.5% Tatars (see Diagram 9). In general, this corresponds with the general ethnic composition of the population of Ukraine, in which Ukrainians comprise

77.8% of the population, Russians 17.3%, Byelorussians 0.6%, Tatars, 0.7%, Bulgarians 0.6%, Jews 0.9% and representatives of other nationalities 2.1%. With regard to distribution by gender, 91% of the elite are men and only 9% are women (see Diagram 10). Thus gender policies have not achieved considerable results thus far. Certain changes, however, are taking place.

Concerning marital status, 52.9% of men are single and 33.7% of women are single (79% of the total number of women). However, it is interesting that the share of single women substantially exceeds the share of single men. The explanation for these fundamental changes in contrast with 2001 is that when the 2001 statistics were compiled, the question about marital status was not mandatory.

An important factor is also regional specificities in the origin of elite representatives. The spheres of activity by region are as follows:

Diagram 9: National composition (in %)

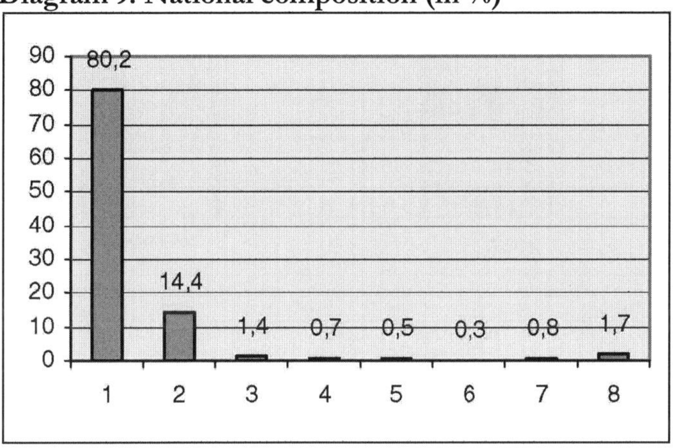

Conventional signs:
1 – Ukrainians; 2 – Russians; 3 – Jews; 4 – Byelorussians; 5 – Crimean Tatars; 6 – Bulgarians; 7 – diasporas; 8 – other nationalities

Representatives of Donets'k and Vinnytsya (accounting for 7% each) are leaders among the representatives of district, regional and local authorities; Kyiv and Kyiv region with (13% and 9%) and Zhytomyr region (7%) dominate among representatives of the highest bodies of power. Donets'k and L'viv regions (accounting for 7% each) dominate among politicians, followed by Dnipropetrovs'k (6%) and Kyiv and Kyiv region (4%). The largest number of judges originates from the Zhytomyr region (10%), Kyiv and Kyiv region (9% and 8%) and the Kharkiv region (6%). An absolute leader among the workers of the mass media is Kyiv with 17% and the Poltava region with 6%.

Diagram 10: Distribution by gender (in %)

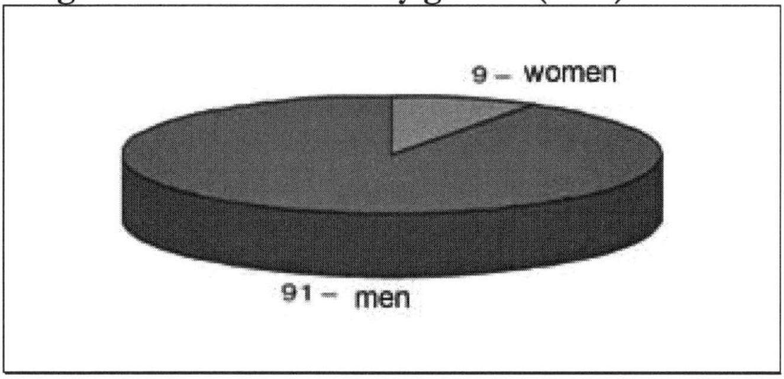

Diagram 11: Marital status (in %)

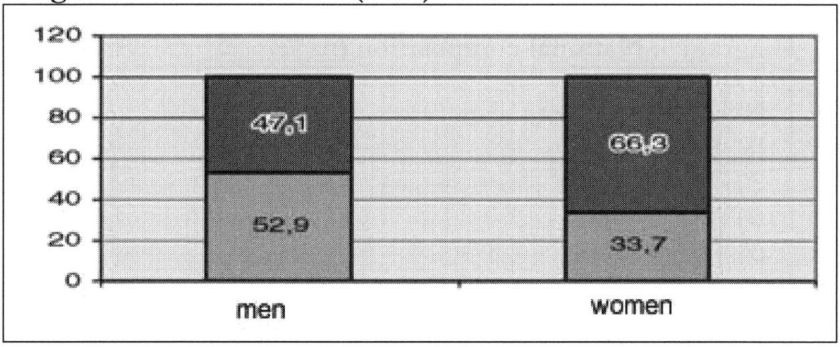

Among representatives of business schools and leaders of enterprise, most people originate from Donets'k and Dnipropetrovs'k (12% and 8% respectively). This can be explained by the fact that these regions are the most industrially developed. Kyiv also belongs to the business centres (8%). Diplomats are represented foremost by Kyiv (24%), followed by Volyn' and Cherkasy regions (6% and 7%). Leaders of various funds are mostly from Kyiv, Kyiv and L'viv regions (13% each). Among trade union workers, 8% originate from Donets'k and Kharkiv each. Among civil society workers, 10% originate from Volyn' and 7% each from Donets'k, Kyiv, Vinnytsya and Zhytomyr regions. 9% of art workers come from Kyiv and Kyiv region each, and 7% each for L'viv, Ivano-Frankivs'k and Poltava regions. Zakarpaya and Chernivtsi regions as well as the Autonomous Republic of Crimea are absolute outsiders in the abovementioned sectors.

Thus quantitative research on the Ukrainian elite conducted in 2005 revealed the following key features: a huge legacy left to the Ukrainian elite by the elite of Soviet Ukraine; an overwhelmingly rural origin of elite representatives; a practically complete correlation between the national composition of elites and the national composition of the population on the whole; high levels of formal education of the establishment with almost no foreign educated elites and even less educated in the west.

The Ukrainian establishment lives in an artificial world of their own making. It is characterised by impunity, with options for the chosen to operate outside any moral or ethical framework and quite often above the law. It is also distinguished by a rather pronounced lack of self-discipline, in spite of the Roman origins of the word elite which stem from the word self-restraint. Being mindful of the etymology of terms, 'aristocracy' is the power of the best, and 'elite' is the chosen one(s).

At the same time, whatever our attitude to the establishment, it is necessary to repeat the well-known words of Y. Stalin to O. Fadeev, 'We have no other writers for you'. On the whole, the overall picture is not very consoling. However, it reflects the real problems faced in the formation of the modern political and administrative elite. That is why it is crucial to think about the mechanisms of elite rotation, possibly its education and suitability for purpose and 'related work'.

The Russian Federation: A Ukrainian Security View

The second factor affecting the national security of Ukraine is the problem associated with post-colonial transition and its external dimension, namely its relation to Russia or, to put it more accurately, the Russian state. Perhaps the most important international factor that impacts on the change of the social-political model of Ukraine is the developments within the Russian Federation. Presently, Ukraine is a sovereign and independent country. However there is a third constituent part in this—autonomy. At present, Ukraine is neither economically, politically nor culturally autonomous. It remains within the limits of post-Soviet space with its inherent models and values.

The problem is not Russia as such but the Russian elite which, in our view, creates disruption. The issue relates to the authoritarian organisation of society and 'draught' state, to use the words of V. Kluchevsky. This includes the ambitions of the great power, the tradition of citizenship, the mobilisation of the population on the basis of imperial ideas and limits on competition to name a few examples. It is a situation that suits Russia, given its enormous resource 'cushion', although it is possible that in a few years this will be exhausted. Such a structure is already disrupting the future of Ukraine. These issues for the most part have been addressed in detail by Russian researchers, in particular, L. Shevtsova, A. Piontkovskiy, V. Gel'man and D. Furman.

This work will attempt to present the author's views about the processes in Russia over the last decade and make certain forecasts in relation to future developments in the Russian Federation and of its actions in relation to Ukraine.

The disintegration of the USSR, as with other empires, did not occur in one moment at the end of 1991. The events of December in that year became only a symbolic milestone in a long process that saw the destruction of the world's largest state. Processes that had been the catalyst for events between 1988 and 1991 had developed in Soviet society during the second half of the 20th century. It is also necessary to examine the processes of the imperial destruction of the USSR not in isolation but as a continuation of certain social trends in the second half of the 20th and the early 21st centuries. These resulted in the collapse of the Russian empire.

According to historians, the cause of the destruction was a failure to modernise following the 'big reforms' of the 1860s. Whilst successes of the liberalisation process are indisputable, these reforms were not able to resolve pressing social problems in the Russian empire. These were most notably the modernisation of rural areas, the transformation of a patriarchal society and the transition to a bourgeois society. Public dissatisfaction caused by defeat or emerging problems resulting from the unexpected success of reforms translated into gradual political radicalisation. In particular, the wave of terror culminating in the civil war of 1918–1922 and its recurrence lasted until it finally faded in the mid 1950s. The social processes of the first half of the 20th century on the territory of the former Russian empire can be characterised as a modernisation crisis not unlike the one in 17th century Germany that resulted in a 30-year war.

A new form of the state, namely the USSR through which an empire was reborn through the Bolshevik Party, had been an effective means of controlling devolutionary trends for only about half a century. For the sake of this new empire, rivers of blood were shed.

The process towards the breaking up of the USSR received new impetus after 1953. Thus the December 1991events have at least a 150-year prehistory. It would therefore have been naïve to have assumed that the resulting inertia would have lasted only a year or two or even ten years given such powerful social processes were at work. Therefore, in many ways the development of post-Soviet societies was occurring during the dissolution of the Russian empire and the Soviet Union.

The situation concerns above all the Russian Federation, and the current leadership of the country realises it. In an address to Russians on the tragedy in Beslan, V. Putin declared on 5 September 2004, 'There have been many tragic pages and difficult challenges in the history of Russia. Today we live in circumstances that emerged after the disintegration of a large and great state, the state which, unfortunately, turned out to be non-functional in a rapidly changing world. But notwithstanding all the difficulties, we succeeded in saving the kernel of this giant, the Soviet Union. And we named a new country the Russian Federation'.[1]

The continued and undivided existence of Soviet geographical space after the Soviet geopolitical break-up became one of the signs of post-imperial trends. Thus a post-imperial and post-colonial paradigm was and remains one of the most effective ways for the analysis of processes in the post-Soviet space. Therefore, the development of the Russian Federation, the central and leading state in this space, is of primary importance in our understanding of the direction and nature of this evolving geopolitical region.

In 2004, the Russian Federation entered a critical stage in its social-political development. The Yeltsin era came to an end. Yeltsin acknowledged the need to create a new political regime in an address after the September 2004

---

1 V. Putin: Segodnya my dolzhny byt' vmeste – tol'ko tak my pobedym Vraga, http://www.kreml.org/news/64834987

events in Beslan.[2] By the end of his first presidential term, V. Putin had ruined the system of checks and balances, carefully built by Boris Yeltsin, and had begun a decisive stage in the race for power, more precisely for the right to determine its form. Russia intensified its foreign policy activity and put pressure on the main source of possible future opposition—oligarchs and their so called 'family' became public manifestations of this.

The failure to democratise Russia and its lack of success in discarding old ways of approaching development in general had become quite apparent by the mid 1990s. At that time, the contradictions among the three main social centres of the 'Russian democratic power' emerged: officials, special services and big owners, otherwise known as 'oligarchs', in the words of Boris Nemtsov.

The main conflict arose between the special services and oligarchs. In the race for power in 1999 and 2000, participation of the bureaucracy was limited. Given their social nature, officials could not be fully removed from power or use their power independently.

The first round of fights, culminating in the events around 'the Xerox box' and the presidential campaign of 1996, ended with the oligarchs victorious and resignations of senior officials of the special services O. Korzhakov and M. Barsukov, supporters of open dictatorship. This victory was brought to life by the creation of 'semibankirshchina' (the rule of seven bankers), which achieved prominence after the election to a second presidential term of an ill Boris Yeltsin in July 1996. However, social disorganisation and public instability created the need for strong personalities and, according to Russian traditions, these personalities needed to be officers of rank.

Fierce conflicts within the oligarchic elite transformed into information wars in 1997 around 'mortgage auctions' and played a critical role in bringing about political instability.

The absence of permanent traditions of interference with the Russians and the Soviet army with politics,[3] the distress of its leadership by a defeat in the first Chechen campaign in 1994–1996 and catastrophic reforms almost instantaneously removed the military from the pool of candidates. Figureheads such as the late Generals O. Lebed' and L. Rokhlin allowed themselves to become nothing more than puppets.

Attempts by the Ministry of Internal Affairs to take power into its hands, mainly through the actions of General A. Kulikov in 1996, were also

2 Yeltsin, B., Ne otkazhemsya ot bukvy i dukha Konstitutsii, http://www.mn.ru/issue.php?2004-35-16

3 The only known case of an active role of the Soviet military in political life was when Marshal G. Zhukov ensured victory for N. Khrushchev over L. Beriya in 1953 and over the 'anti-party group' of V. Molotov, G. Malenkov and others in 1956. However, this very act of G. Zhukov became the principal reason of his resignation and falling into disgrace at once after the final strengthening of power by N. Khrushchev in 1957.

unsuccessful because of exceptionally unfavourable circumstances and the unpreparedness of Russia's internal affairs bodies for political games at the highest levels.

All of this defined the exceptional role of the special services and their personnel, who in modern Russia are named 'chekisty', sometimes with the addition of an epithet 'orthodox'. The role of 'civilian' special services in the political system of Russia remained exceptionally important during most of the soviet period, however, not so in other republics of the USSR. In the spring and summer of 1953, one *chekisty* group led by L. Beriya aimed at taking over the highest power in the USSR. After this defeat, KGB workers and the structures that replaced them in the Russian Federation obtained vast experience in influencing public policy and, apart from great ambitions, had sufficient motivation. On the whole, this theme needs careful and independent research.

Already in 1997, a certain consensus had emerged between oligarchs and *chekisty*. As noted above, compromise among the Russian elites was facilitated by the elections of 1996, which almost materialised the ghost of a civil war. Events around 'the Xerox box' were not to repeat themselves. The 'semibankirshchina' set certain economic order but needed support for power.

The basis of consensus among the elite at that time was following approximately the distribution of power: political power belonged to the *chekisty* and economic power to the oligarchs. It was precisely this compromise that allowed the quiet resolution of the problem of succession. During 1998–1999, a sort of presidential casting—described in detail by Boris Yeltsin in the mentioned interview for *Moscow News*—was taking place. It is public knowledge that V. Putin was the winner of this casting.

The consensus did not last for long, almost five years in all. According to the leading ideologist of this informal agreement, G. Pavlovskiy, in public life this consensus was based on 'the attempts to freeze' Russia (paraphrased from K.Pobedonostsev). Revival of the Russian policy as a result of this consensus opened the same perspectives to the 'democratic princeps', which at one time were used by the first Roman princeps Guy Octavian August. Conditions favourable to shadow political activity emerged and bureaucratic structures were consolidated.

Multimillionaires became politically defenceless before the state, which they had handed over to the *chekisty*. The checks and balances as personified in the head of Presidential Administrator O. Voloshin and Prime Minister M. Kasyanov had their 'guarantee resource'. By the time the more politically savvy oligarchs understood their time was coming to an end, it was too late. The M. Khodorkovskiy case and the propagandist campaign around the resignation of O. Voloshin unfolded in the mass media close to the 'family'. Other developments also confirmed that in autumn 2003 the culmination of the conflict occurred. Precisely at that time a collision of 'bulldogs under the blanket' took place. A Russian journalist Y. Tregubova[4] painted an interesting but rather biased and emotive picture of this collision. The regime of Putin took tangible form after the elections in March 2004 and the events in Beslan in September of the same year, when he proclaimed the basic direction of political reforms.

In Russia, during V. Putin's first term, the revival of a political regime called 'the Russian power'[5] by Y. Pivovarov took place. It was characterised by the leader legitimising the state through his high ratings. This assumed a specific guise via a disproportionate significance on the special services and their employees, coined by M. Patrushev, 'the new nobility'. According to O. Kryshtanovskaya, leading Russian specialist on the elite, the share of '*siloviki*' (top brass), mainly *chekisty*, increased from 13% in 1999 to 42% in 2008 and to 70%[6] in other sectors to Bonapartist characteristics of the Russian regime. Above all, relative political autonomy of the bureaucracy and the state on the whole became apparent.[7] Virtual political technologies played a key role in the establishment and functioning of the new Russian regime. Some researchers even characterised the late Yeltsin, early Putin regime as 'mediacracy'.

The victory of *chekisty* in no way meant the return to the practice of 'remove and divide' but the basic contours of managed democracy in the Russian Federation became more evident. A 'defence' system headed by 'grey' and collective '*Pobedonostsev*' formed. The establishment of the populist regime with an orthodox *chekist* face, defined ideologically by V. Surkov in the concept 'sovereign democracy', occurred.

This concerns the perception of social reality not only by the ruling elite but also by ordinary Russian citizens. There is also an indisputable connection between the consciousness of the masses and that of the elite. Quite often propagandists begin to believe in their own inventions and that the people persuade the leaders, who are much too authoritarian, to operate in accordance with their own understanding of the world.

What inspires heroes to 'fight for it', leaving their homes 'in the native land of long-suffering'? Supporters of the notion put forward by prominent Russian Leninist Historian Mikhail Pokrovskiy and American Sovietologist Richard Pipes that Russians are a big merchant people would argue money and 'gold'. They would be partly correct. Others would argue power and 'sword'.

---

4 Tregubova Y., Bayki kremlevskogo diggera, Moscow: Ad marginem, 2004.

5 Pivovarov Y., Russkaya politicheskaya kul'tura i political culture, Pro et contra, Summer, 2002.

6 Kryshtanovskaya O., Rossiyskaja elita na perekhode, http://www.polit.ru/lectures/2008/07/31/rus_elita.html.

7 Marks K., Vosemnadtsatoye bryumera Lui Bonaparta, http://www.1917.com/Marxism/Marx/18-Brumera/index.html.

Experts on Russian authoritarianism and imperial aspirations would not be mistaken either. Supporters of psychoanalytic theories would suggest national complexes, being mindful of the analytical constructs of 'grandmother Austria'. They would be right as well. These are all good answers but by no means exhaustive. We do not intend to identify the actual reasons for the course of leadership by the Russian state. Our aim is to reconstruct those structures that became the armour of a modern fighter on the Russian ideological front.

To examine history first, for more than seventy years Marxist-Leninism dominated Russia in a canonical version sanctified by Josef Stalin. This can be found in the theoretical chapter of the 'Short Course of History of the All-Russian Bolshevic (Communist) Party'. According to V. Lenin, any monopoly leads to decay. The general level of thinking about a man and society in the Soviet Union firmly reflected this position at the beginning of the 20th century.

Notwithstanding the efforts of ideological departments, humanities and social sciences were only a glimmer within the mainstream of the USSR's correct teaching. Prominent humanities scholars worked on certain cases like semiotics, sociology and the like (M. Bakhtin, Y. Illenkov, Y. Lotman, O. Zinoviev, A. Gurevich, to name a few).

But these rays of light did not create the weather in 'the dark kingdom'. Supporters of marginal approaches to the modern humanities dominant at the beginning of the 20th century prevailed alongside and under the mask of Marxist conformists as it became apparent afterwards. An intellectual climate was formed by two main groups, namely, conditional westernizers, 'Liberals', and Slavophiles, 'Russian Party'.

Westernizers, the mainstream representatives of the Russian culture, oriented themselves to liberal values and approaches perceived as the new Holy Scriptures or rather 'The Capital'. On reading their texts or listening to their ardent speeches, it is not John Stuart Mill or Friedrich von Hayek who are brought to mind but rather priest Avakum or 'furious Vissarion' (Belinskiy). Understanding of liberal and other ideas was in no way characterised by depth and excessive attention to the form, which in previous centuries had resulted in ritualism.

After the Second World War, Slavophiles grew up on a strange mixture of ideas from Europe originally but substantially modified in the 'land of birch printed cotton', among which classical geopolitics and various conspiracy theories with noticeable racist touches occupied the main place. 'The patriots' and 'the Russian Party' united around the magazines *Nash Sovremennik* and *Molodaya Gvardiya* as well as the Central Committee of the de facto All-Union Leninist Young Communist League. They traced their ideological genesis to the ultra-conservative branch of Slavophiles through the Black Hundreds (Russian imperialistic nationalists), part of whom acknowledged the Bolshevik revolution in 1917 as a national phenomenon. For those interested in how 'the Russian party' developed, there is a rich source of unbiased work by the Russian scholar N. Mitrokhin.[8]

In 'the evil 90s' when, according to A. Yakovlev, 'the solid earth shifted', the change of views in the Russian sciences about man and society as a basic source for ideological constructions began. While 'Tsar Boris' requested researchers to create the national idea, the adoption of modern scientific achievements took place in Russia with the assistance of the G. Soros Fund and other western donor organisations. The ideas of 'the patriots', who were given the pseudonym of 'red-brown', were marginalised. It became unfashionable to read their newspapers, above all *Sovetskaya Rossiya* (Sovraska) and 'the newspaper of spiritual opposition', *Zavtra*. However, it was a strange time for Russia when practically everything was published. Works of great liberals were published together with works of no less prominent conservatives and even of obscure types. It was possible to purchase books by Alexis de Tocqueville and M. Leontyev in kiosks and shops. A. Hitler and A. Rozenberg were also available for sale.

Times changed after the second Chechen war and the election of V. Putin. At the beginning of the 21st century, a Russian version of liberal-democratic ideas that had been adopted non-critically was rendered lacking and 'tsarist disgrace' for supporters of these ideas. This freed up space for the Russian presidential 'throne'. Numerous supporters of 'the fifth empire' and 'Russian power' occupied the 'holy place' similar to 'the nightingale of the General Staff', still Soviet and talentless publicist and writer A. Prokhanov, television political scientists S. Markov, M. Leontyev and A. Pushkov, for example. New 'persons of dominant influence', even more zealous than those of the late Soviet era, began to argue 'the need for autocratic power and the beauty of the whip'.

Putin, as the second president of Russia, has played the role of arbiter among different groups of the elite rather than autocrat, a policy that gradually intensified ahead of the presidential elections. However, the height of this game of contradictions took place at the end of 2007. An illustrative example of this was the scandal of Autumn 2007 surrounding the arrest of General A. Bul'bov and the publication by V. Cherkesov of an article 'A soldier should not be a businessman', where the leading role of Cheka officials in the recent history of Russia was proved. According to many commentators, it was precisely this event that led to the reshuffling of the higher echelons of the Russian government after the arrival of D. Medvedev—in particular, the dismissal of V. Cherkesov as head of one of the most powerful Russian special services, the State Drugs Control.

8 Mitrokhin N., Russkaya partiya, http://www.situation.ru/app/j_art_456.htm, http://www.situation.ru/app/j_art_458.htm.

'The 2008 Problem'—the question of transfer of power from Putin to his successor of Medvedev—was resolved on the basis of a fundamentally different model. On 14 April 2008, the Congress of 'United Russia' took place in Moscow. It became one of the seminal events that shaped President Medvedev's political regime.

On the same day, changes were introduced in the statutes of the party. They foresaw the creation of the position of party chairman, which could be occupied by a person not belonging to the party. On 15 April, Vladimir Putin agreed to become the chairman of 'United Russia' and also confirmed his desire to become the Prime Minister of the Russian Federation. In a speech, the former Russian president defined the tasks for development both of the party and the country. Putin's leading role was even more openly outlined in his programmatic speech in the State Duma, when he was appointed as the head of government. The new prime minister of the Russian Federation had in fact proclaimed the presidential message.

Thus, the character of the new Russian political regime became apparent. Authoritarian models with one dominant party with their roots in the Russian Federation had functioned for a sufficiently long time in a few Latin American countries in the 20th century.[9] Mexico can serve as a classical example of such a system from the 1920s–1990s, when the Institutional-Revolutionary party dominated the political life of the country for about 70 years.

In describing the experience of countries of 'the third world', political science confirms that authoritarian systems with one dominant party are far more stable than personal dictatorships. Their period of control can usually be measured in decades. Accordingly, subject to oil and gas prices remaining high, the present Russian regime has every chance of demonstrating enviable longevity.

At the same time, however, with external stability such a model has one considerable defect: near total corruption generates an overall inflexibility of the state machine and deepens the orientation of the economy towards the exploitation of natural resources.

The current occupants of the Kremlin understand this problem, which is why they plan to extend their arsenal of defence for the regime. They are doing this in particular through the instruments of political justice. Therefore, on 14 December 2008, the government of the Russian Federation submitted a bill to the State Duma proposing the exemption of crimes against the state (high treason, espionage, etc.) from trial by jury. The bill also paves the way for a substantial expansion of the corresponding articles of the Criminal Code. In particular, there is a proposal to amend the code to waive the necessity to prove participation in hostile activity against Russian Federation security. The effect

---

9 Gelman V., Transformatsiya rossiyskoy politicheskoy sistemy, http://www.polit.ru/lectures/2008/03/14/gelman.html.

of this will be to allow practically any collaboration with foreign structures to qualify as espionage or high treason. Thus the legal preconditions for repressive support of the Russian authoritarian regime are being formed.

However, other signals are coming from the Kremlin. For example, on 29 January 2009, President Medvedev met with the ex-president of the USSR, M. Gorbachev and the editor-in-chief of *Novaya gazeta*, D. Muratov. The official reason for the meeting was to express condolences to the paper's management for the murder of journalist A. Baburova. However, according to some commentators, in particular V. Portnikov, this follows steps taken in the early Gorbachev years as an attempt to 'flirt with society' during economically difficult times. Consequently 'détente' is not eliminated either.

Notwithstanding the above, Russian foreign policy has clear strategic goals, the achievement of which requires proper resources. At the same time, the populist character of the Russian political regime greatly complicates the transition to a traditional way of decreasing standards of living of the general population that never speaks of limiting the incomes of the elite.

The lack of possibilities for realisation of ambitious foreign policy, as well as of real economic and personal integration of the Russian establishment in the structures of the global world, will lead to certain contradictions in the actions of the Russian leadership.

On the one hand, the political line of the Russian Federation in relationships with the West will go through, depending on the economic situation, periods of gradual detente or vice versa. On the other hand, the policy in relation to weaker countries will become tougher and sometimes even 'adventurous'. These features of foreign policy have already become apparent in the territories of the former USSR, in particular during the August 2008 military conflict in the Caucasus.

Incidentally, this tendency emerged at the beginning of the 1990s, as was noted in the public lecture given by the External Secret Service of the Russian Federation (then headed by Y. Primakov) entitled 'Russia and the CIS: does the position of the West require it to change?'

The necessary pre-condition for the realisation of the strategic plans of the Russian Federation is the establishment of complete control over the post-Soviet space. A model, possibly imposed subconsciously, that achieves this kind of desired future for the territories under Kremlin influence is the former 'socialist camp' or to be precise, the Brezhnev doctrine whereby countries that are allies of Moscow enjoy limited sovereignty. This allows the Kremlin the right of veto in important state decisions of such satellite countries, resulting in its domination of their economies.

Practical steps in relation to this task have been taken by the Kremlin for a few years already. The American paradigm of 'the fight against international terrorism' had considerable influence on the mechanisms and means of dismantling the former Soviet republics. The issue is about Russian attempts to reproduce the American global policy within the confines of the former USSR. The actions of the Russian Federation have been determined by traditional, Moscow, complexes in relation to former 'sister-republics' and cherished by the post-Soviet elite for the last seventeen years. It is enough to remember the CIS summits at the level of head of state and diplomacy 'without ties'.

The fight against 'colour' revolutions, which convinced the Kremlin about the necessity of actively working with non-governmental organisations and the mass media, had a considerable influence on Russian policy.

The Russian Federation's influence against the CIS extended from economic, namely energy, to pressure and activation of the 'fifth column' and the use of force. At that time, Russia had developed other means of wielding influence over the post-Soviet states—the events against Georgia in the Pankis canyon in 2002–2003 being one such example. When this failed, Russia changed its emphasis over the following five years. It chose instead to exert its influence via economic means, focussing on the fuel-energy sector.

However, non-military methods of exerting control were also employed, the building of the Tuzla dam in autumn 2003 being a case in point.

Tuzla became the final rehearsal ground ahead of the presidential elections in 2004 in Ukraine. The activation of pro-Russian forces during Ukrainian independence peaked precisely when the situation around Tuzla deteriorated. The issue at stake was not so much about who favoured the developing of relations between an independent Ukraine and Russia, but about those who openly supported the expansionist policy of the Kremlin.

The following events confirmed to the public the impotence of these forces. Tuzla united almost all Ukrainian political figures around the idea of sovereignty and territorial integrity of their state. This incident showed the presence of a principal psychological conflict between Ukrainian and the Russian ruling elite. According to the political scientist V. Palamarchuk, Tuzla almost divided the 'Siamese twins', that is the establishments of the two countries.

It is difficult to disagree with British expert James Sherr who argues that events around Tuzla should be considered as 'battle reconnaissance' and a test of the reaction of the Ukrainian state and the West to openly unfriendly actions of the Russian Federation. The idea by A. Hal'chyns'kyy that the purpose of these actions was 'the intention of Moscow to make impossible the process of Euro-Atlantic integration of Ukraine at any price' through the creation of a territorial dispute should be mentioned. The economic basis for the construction of the dam—from the problems of the Kerch channel to the creation of an ammonia terminal—should not be underestimated.

After Kosovo's proclamation of independence, the Kremlin activated 'frozen' conflicts to exert its influence on post-Soviet countries. Georgia was the basic target of the Russian Federation's foreign policy following the victory of the 'tulip revolution' in 2003 and M. Saakashvili's ascent to power.

The next episode was the events in Georgia in August 2008. The Russian's analysis confirmed that the game had ended forever or, in any case, for a long time. Real life had begun. Russia has revealed, in one of the worst historical traditions, that the only right it respects is the right of force. It is an obvious result of the development of Russian society and, in particular, its elite.

Tbilisi provoked Moscow by attacking South Ossetia, however, this provocation was expected and facilitated in Bilokamyana. A thesis about the August 2008 conflict in Georgia as 'the mirror effect' must be mentioned here: basically that Saakashvili followed Putin in beginning the war under the banner of 'the restoration of the constitutional regime', while Medvedev was at war with Georgia using the rhetoric of George Bush junior of 'enforcing peace' and 'stopping genocide'.

The Russians carried out their policy line quite consistently except for one important point. According to an interesting observation by a Russian opposition journalist Y. Latinina, the Georgian military and police were called fighters on the television channels of the Russian Federation, thus denying the legitimacy of the Georgian authorities.[10]

There is a lot of talk about morals. It is an exercise in futility as neither Mikhail Saakashvili nor Vladimir Putin followed the rules governing morality in their practical activity. Those who think otherwise should refer to the works of the great Niccolo Machiavelli who in the 16th century argued that rulers should be judged in accordance with special criteria.

The highest value of the Westphalian system and its successors—that is, the state sovereignty of Georgia—was crudely violated by the Russian military. In this situation, the actual impotence of the global community became apparent.

Therefore, the range of possible methods to exert influence and control will increase until such time that someone will be able to explain the futility and danger of the uncontrollable use of force.

The Russian-Georgian armed conflict swiftly turned into a battle for the elimination of M. Saakashvili. The conduct of Europe and the US in the conflict confirmed that Mikhail Saakashvili operated at his own risk, counting on the classic adage 'the winners are not judged'. No one in Tbilisi had considered the possibility of defeat.

---

10 By the way, the same can be said about Ukraine (in the article 'A Yellow-Blue Land-lease' on the site 'RPMonitor' of 14 October 2008 by a popular Russian publicist M. Kalashnikov). The following was said about possible transfer of the American battleships to the navy of Ukraine: 'Should We be Afraid of the Transfer of the American Battleships to the Ukrainian Nationalists?'

The Georgian regime does not deserve the nickname 'puppet', a term commonly used by the Russian Federation. The most probable question is one about self-confidence and in no way about conspiracy. How could there be secrets and plots when Tbilisi and Moscow used every opportunity to openly inform the world of their plans?

The primary objective of the Russian Federation in this conflict is obvious: it is to make itself appear great for the first time in twenty years. The effect of this need to feel powerful again overwhelmed all expectation of loss: both real (battle and economic) and imaginary, including in the West.

It was necessary to show the world that the Kremlin would stop at nothing to protect its interests, particularly, 'the privileged zones of interest'. The conflict can actually be viewed as a punitive operation against a mutinous vassal. Therefore, another task was to bring down the extremely defiant Georgian regime as well as to intimidate Ukraine and other 'disobedient' neighbours.

The role of Russia's energy policy in all of this cannot be discounted. Intrusion into Georgia was aimed at establishing control over oil pipelines from Azerbaijan to Turkey.

Finally, maybe most importantly, it was the need to test the West: what ultimately were its capacities?

Ukraine as the key country in the post-Soviet space

This rather ordinary notion does not diminish its practical importance. An advantageous geographical position, transit resources, the richest deposits of minerals and black soils are Ukraine's wealth and simultaneous sorrow. Ukraine possesses a gold card, a joker in the Eurasian geopolitical pack. The results of the next round of the Big Game depend in great measure on whose side Kyiv will play.

For the Russian Federation, the final loss of control over Ukraine will, in the medium term, mean the loss of influence over Byelorussia and, consequently, limit Russia's presence in Asia and the potential to build direct and strategic relations with the EU. In the long term, this will lead to even more negative and possibly catastrophic consequences for the Russian Federation; particularly the demographic problems within the Russian Federation and a gradual decrease of its share of the Slav population.

It is simultaneously impossible to ignore the 'demonstration effect', that is, the successful democratisation of Ukraine, which destroys the prospects of the authoritarian regime in Russia.

This in particular determines the orientation and impact of the Russian Federation's distinctly imperial policy towards Ukraine.[11] The question is not about another accusation directed against Moscow but about foreseeing a series of measures directed at the formation of a loyal elite and its take-over by political and economic means. This strategy, known as indirect imperial management, was effectively used for over three thousand years. Therefore, the Kremlin policy primarily aims to form and then use loyalist groups within the Ukrainian establishment to achieve its policy.

The loss by Ukraine of its formal independence is unlikely but in the very apt words of one insightful German, the issue is about the formation of a one-sided dependence, which has no prospects. This dependence leads not to development but to a failure to develop. Those representatives of the Ukrainian elite who expect that Ukraine will occupy the place it had in the USSR, 'the second among equal' in 'the liberal empire', are destined to rapid and deep disappointment. It is sufficient to look at the Russian media that acquired a closed and occasionally xenophobic attitude over the last years to prove the accuracy of the last opinion.

In reality, this is an interesting paradox of Russian policy: imperial strategy, imperial methods and closed ideology. The traditional imperial methods of indirect management are currently being used not by an imperial power open to the world and embarking on expansion but rather by a state defending itself.[12] Russia carries out a strategic retreat, cultivating a closed, ideally hermetic, public consciousness within the country.

The Euro-Atlantic integration of Ukraine is not the reason but a catalyst for the deterioration of relations with Russia. The matter is not about NATO, the USA or the EU but the departure of Ukraine from the post imperial space and the impact of a successful and democratic Ukraine on Russian society. At the moment there is no effective system of mutual relations between our neighbouring, friendly but independent countries. In discussing relations between Ukraine and Russia, the authors are mindful of how imperial Britain actively protected Ottawa from Washington's attempts to absorb the latter during the second half of the 19th and early 20th century—a somewhat forgotten fact. Kyiv must create an effective system of cooperation with the Russian Federation otherwise it will be created for Ukraine without its input. Then, as has previously been noted, the most likely scenario may be the transformation of Ukraine into a kind of 'Socialist Poland' that existed between the 1950s and 1970s. This will involve the establishment in Ukraine of an authoritarian, nominally pro-Kremlin regime for a few years, whereupon we will return to the current situation but with a different principal element.

---

11 Kappeler A., Rosiya yak polietnichna imperiya, L'viv: Vyd-vo Ukr. Katolyts'koho un-tu, 2005.

12 Compare with the central thesis of the newspaper *Zavtra* on 'defence consciousness'.

Ukrainian society and elite will become inundated with deep prejudice and vigilance not just against the state of the Russian Federation but to Russian society. And in this phobia there can be nothing good either for Ukraine or its neighbours.

To exercise its influence on Ukraine, the Kremlin has created a branched and multilevel system. This consists of various structures and organisations, which engage the resources of the presidential administration of the Russian Federation, the government of Russia and its separate departments, as well as the Russian special services, the State Duma and executive power of the Federation's units. Resources of Russian non-governmental organisations have been actively exploited over the last years, with the most active among them being the Institute of the CIS Countries with its well-financed Ukrainian representative office.

A special role in the realisation of this policy is also played by the *Russkiy mir* fund, which supports the humanitarian arm of Russia's foreign policy and provides support for projects related to the development of Russian culture outside the Russian Federation.[13] The numerous visits to Ukraine of Russian political and public figures, in particular of those radically opposed to Ukraine, cannot be ignored.

Russian pressure on Ukraine is exerted in three basic ways. Firstly, Moscow uses its potential as a basic supplier of fuel-energy resources.

Secondly, the deliberate anti-Ukrainian propaganda campaign carried out by the Kremlin and with the active participation of the special services of the Russian Federation has intensified.

Thirdly, Moscow is concentrating efforts on the Crimea, attempting to wield influence on the course of events in the Autonomous Republic of Crimea (ARC) through the realisation of a policy of managed instability. Thus the

[13] On 21 July 2007, the President of the Russian Federation V. Putin decreed the creation of the fund 'Russkiy mir' tasked with supporting the humanitarian dimension of Russian foreign policy, providing support for projects related to the development of Russian culture in foreign countries, etc. Co-founders of the fund were the Ministry of Foreign Affairs and the Ministry of Education of the Russian Federation. A known Russian political scientist V. Nikonov was appointed as the president of the fund (the executive director of the board) and L. Verbitska, Rector of Saint Petersburg University and a friend of V. Putin's wife, as the chairman of the board of trustees. Among the partners of the fund are not only such respected institutions as the Pushkin House or the Institute of Russian of the Russian Academy of Sciences but also the Institute of the CIS Countries, which speaks about the diversification of interests of this establishment. In fact, the question is about the establishment in Russia of a system like the British Council, Goethe Institute or L'Institut Francais, a powerful instrument in the advancement of Russian soft power beyond the borders of the federation. Currently, the fund concentrates on efforts related to the advancement of Russian as the language of inter-ethnic communication in the CIS countries. However, an expansion of the range of its interests and active participation of the fund's institutions in the realisation of the Russian foreign-policy goals, and not only for the Ministry of Foreign Affairs, can be expected.

ultimate goal is to turn the peninsula into an important mechanism for influencing the policy of Kyiv.

Hence the Black Sea Fleet of the Russian Federation plays a key role in the realisation of Russian policy vis-à-vis Ukraine. Activities there have increased as 2017 approaches and herald the expiry date for agreements in relation to the placement of the Russian military naval bases in Ukraine.

We will attempt to describe these directions in detail. The key element in the realisation of a superpower energy project is the expansion into energy markets, particularly the infrastructure of European countries. Ukraine's geographical location combined with its developed infrastructure force Moscow to concentrate its efforts on establishing control over the transit capacities of Ukraine.

'The gas wars' initiated by the Kremlin are an effective lever of influence over the political and economic processes in Ukraine. The main consequences of these have been:

- Decreased control over socio-political processes and capabilities of the state authorities, emergence of conflict between the authorities and Ukrainian businesses, above all big business;
- Increased dissatisfaction by the population of Ukraine with the leadership of the state, decrease in public support for the state authorities leading to radicalisation of political life in the state;
- The influence of electoral options to facilitate more support for the pro-Russian political forces or forces that are viewed as such by the leadership of the Russian Federation; and
- Damage to Ukraine's positive international image as a reliable economic partner and actor in the EU energy security policy.

A mass political information campaign has also been an important factor in the Russian Federation wielding influence on the political processes in Ukraine. Action by various Russian and Ukrainian persons and organisations are synchronised to an extent and serve to confirm a high level of management in the anti-Ukrainian political information campaign.

The Kremlin, even in the official statements of the Ministry of Foreign Affairs, overtly exploits the motto of the protection of humanitarian and political rights for the Russian and Russian-language population in Ukraine. Accusations against Kyiv in the distortion and re-writing of history intensify. A campaign about the non-recognition of the Holodomor and restoration of historical justice concerning OUN-UPA, which is interpreted as the resurrection of fascism, continues. What is often surprising is that in reality the issue is more about personalities and the reactions of those who have been offended and not about a balanced policy.

Thus, according to V. Nebozhenko, such a passionate reaction is caused by the fact that Russian politicians appreciate the nationalist character of Kyiv's policy relating to the restoration of its historical past. They can also foresee the enormous potential, if this policy is appropriately applied, as well as realise what difficulties are in store for Russia if it fails to recognise this.

Russian propagandists take advantage of increasing xenophobia. The rise in the number of racist, including anti-Semitic attacks in Ukraine by skinheads, is notable. International influence on these attacks cannot be cannot be entirely discounted. The campaign of xenophobia is propagated by leading state and non-state Russian owned television channels, which broadcast to a wide audience abroad including Ukraine. Other Russian editions and branches in Ukraine as well as the pro-Russian Ukrainian media, serve as a propaganda resource. A broad system of pro-Russian sites created in Ukraine is online.

In order to influence the socio-political situation in Ukraine, Russia utilises existing civil political pro-Russian organisations while initiating the creation of new organisations in Ukraine, including those with radical and separatist views.

Attempts to consolidate and coordinate the activity of pro-Russian autonomic structures, primarily in southeast Ukraine, continue. This concerns various Cossack groups and the Eurasian Union of Young People, for example.

The Kremlin attempts to use Orthodox organisations, in particular radical elements, which were condemned by the Assembly of Hierarchs of the Ukrainian Orthodox Church (Moscow Patriarchate) in late 2007.

Russia is also raising the *Rusyn* issue. The alleged need to determine the status of *Carpathian Rus* and defence of its 'religion and culture' has seen increased activity by representatives of Russian non-governmental organisations. Lately, this problem has become further aggravated by the participation of certain Ukrainian political and business groups with obvious criminal roots.

The third key direction of pressure concerns the Crimea. There Russia attempts to convert the peaceful peninsula into an area of managed instability, making tensions rise or fall by command from the Kremlin. Every means is used: from instigation of xenophobic, anti-Tatar and anti-Western views to speculation on the social-economic problems of Ukraine.

Key features of the region enable the Kremlin to pursue such a policy. In the first place, the presence of a considerable group (290'000 persons) of Crimean Tatars in Crimea, whose cultural-historical, national and religious traditions are quite different from that of the majority, is important. This group returned to Crimea in an organised way only one and a half decades ago. Therefore, the ground is fertile for the emergence of inter-ethnic and inter-religious conflict on the peninsula.

Second, there is the unique character of the Crimean establishment and the direct contacts it established with Moscow, bypassing Kyiv, in the Soviet years. It also received a privileged status as a result of the unofficial status of the South coast and above all because Yalta, the summer capital of the USSR, is located there.

Third, the Crimean peninsula is a unique region of Ukraine, where ethnic Russians constitute a small but absolute majority.

Fourth, the Russian Black Sea Fleet is stationed on the peninsula in Sevastopol. The Black Sea Fleet of the Russian Federation, though a non-military one, ensures Russia's presence in Crimea and in Ukraine. It can carry out tactical manoeuvres in the Black Sea, and did so during the Russian-Georgian conflict. At present, the Black Sea Fleet is not robust enough to ensure that operational-strategic operations are carried out. The fleet is no longer a threat to the 6th (Mediterranean) fleet of the naval forces of the USA, or to the military fleet of Turkey.

However, the fleet carries out important political tasks effectively enough. It is important to remember that there is an intelligence department as well as special purpose units within the fleet, which do not passively observe the social-political developments on the peninsula.

The numerous memorial plaques, busts and other symbols in honour of Russian generals and admirals in Sevastopol cannot be ignored. It is evidence of the work by the memorial group of the Black Sea Fleet, which creates symbols of the Russian presence in Crimea.

The slightest presence of the Black Sea Fleet in Sevastopol clearly speaks of the fact that the Russian empire is there, has not disappeared and hopes to remain forever.

All of this is nourished by the pro-imperial mood among the Russophone population of the peninsula. For what better television scenes than the parades of the Black Sea seaman of Russia in Sevastopol and the stationing of ships under the St. Andrew's flag at the Graf wharf to assert the firmness of Russian positions on the Black seaside?

Therefore, the Black Sea Fleet is not immune as another potentially powerful source of corruption in Ukraine. The fleet is based almost on the south bank of Crimea, and consequently the territory of its units can be used not only for the deployment of rockets and radars, but also for the placement of more peaceful structures, such as dachas.

Given the arguments in favour of retaining its military presence, the likelihood of Moscow applying all instruments of pressure on Ukraine in order to extend the agreements on the stationing of the Black Sea Fleet after 2017 is great.

The Black Sea Fleet is a military structure therefore the need for its presence can be substantiated by arguments in favour of neutralising military threats. There is a temptation therefore to exacerbate the emerging conflict, in which the units of the Black Sea Fleet would play a peacemaking role. The perceived conflict would most probably be escalated on inter-ethnic or inter-religious grounds rather than military ones.

The presence of two communities with different religious and national traditions in Crimea, whose representatives are involved in the fight for the distribution of limited and valuable resources, including land, lends itself to such a scenario. It is worth remembering the events of 2006 in Bakhchisarai and the role of pro-Russian organisations. The stories and analyses on ORT and RTR television channels consistently advanced ideas about the future Crimean Kosovo (Chechnya). We should not forget other interests either—specifically tourism, which traditionally relies on competition with Crimea regions of the Russian Caucasus including Sochi, the fight against international Islamic terrorism and 'appeasement of the Northern Caucasus'. Therefore, while the Black Sea Fleet is based in Crimea, socio-political stability in the longer term within the autonomy can be expected and, should that change, the converse will apply.

The question about the withdrawal of the Black Sea Fleet is a principal one from yet another perspective. The decision to adopt and implement the re-deployment of the main base of the Black Sea Fleet on Russian territory will most probably mean a number of things. The recognition by the Kremlin of Ukraine's right to conduct a truly independent foreign policy and Russia's renunciation of plans to limit the sovereignty of Ukraine.

Thus, without casting aspersions on the legitimacy of the deployment of the Black Sea Fleet on Ukraine's territory until 2017, it is necessary to begin a plan of action. This should involve the development and implementation of gradual and consistent mechanisms aimed at regulating all aspects of the withdrawal of Russian troops upon the termination of the terms in the relevant agreements. Namely, the decision of the National Security and Defence Council of Ukraine of 16 May 2008 'On measures ensuring the development of Ukraine as a naval state' (Decree of the President of Ukraine of 20th May 2008 No. 463) and the Decree of the President of Ukraine of 26 December 2008 No. 1204 'On additional measures on social-economic development of the city Sevastopol.'

A further thorny issue relates to the state border of Ukraine with that of the Russian Federation. The main question is about the delimitation and legal regulation of the waters of the state border in the areas of the Azov and Black seas, in particular the Kerch channel. However, it should be noted that it serves Russia's interests to keep the questions of the boundary unresolved so it can be used as a lever for further pressure on Ukraine.

Finally, while dealing with authoritarian Moscow, it should be clear that the strategy of its expansionism is usually built on the principle 'knock on all doors, some of them will open'. Success in one direction results in an immediate concentration of resources on it and an ensuing increase of pressure.

Russian researcher Y. Zubkova, who studied the Stalinist project of absorption of the Baltic countries in 1939–1940, notes that Y. Stalin had only a general awareness about the strategic purpose of the policy aimed at the USSR's annexation of Lithuania, Latvia and Estonia. The detailed plan of its realisation was non-existent. 'Everything was created on the run', and decisions were taken on an ad hoc basis.[14] The analysis of current Russian policy in the post-Soviet space confirms that an algorithm does indeed operate. This needs to be clearly understood as Kyiv develops its policy in relation to Russia.

---

14 Zubkova Y., Stalinskiy proekt dlya Pribaltiki, http://www.polit.ru/lectures/2009/01/13/pribalt.html.

NATO and the National Security of Ukraine

An important consequence of the double problem (that is, establishment of the local elite and the process of decolonisation) is a progressive ruin of the state institutes of Ukraine. The state turns into a toothless tiger and so anything is possible both from inside and outside. This is especially dangerous in conditions of integration of Ukraine into the current global competition space.

The reason for ruin is the impotence of those forming the state, the problem of the elite, insufficient state-building traditions and incomplete decolonisation. It is difficult to build a truly independent Ukraine on the imperial tradition inherited from the Russian empire and the USSR. Owing to centuries of non-state history, the national tradition is to this day unfortunately not robust enough.

The stability of the political system during Leonid Kuchma's presidency was due to the recreating of Soviet schemes of management. Kuchma and his administration breathed life into dead institutions. It helped to solve problems of the time effectively enough but did not provide a long-term strategic vision.

The disintegration of these institutions continues from the time of the 'Orange Revolution'. This explains the spread of corruption because structures that degenerate are already corrupt; corruption in such a system is not an exception but merely a method of survival.

The situation is difficult but not hopeless. The search for a president who would accelerate the development of Ukraine has lasted seventeen years. Hope was placed on the oligarchs who were expected to establish order; bureaucrats, after the 'Orange Revolution' would do the same for civil society and the middle class.

Presently, the middle class is already a powerful player in Kyiv and cities with more than a million citizens. In other regions, however, the situation is a little different. Conditional on the economy growing, the middle class will become stronger and will become more powerful players on a national scale in another ten to fifteen years. Similar processes took place in the second half of the 20th century in Latin America (Brazil and Argentina). However, this process lasted roughly four stormy decades and was characterised by the rule of military dictatorships and the development and decline of populist movements.

The number of informal organisations has grown rapidly. Besides having a positive role of asserting pressure on the state and business, they sometimes acquire a radical character. On the one hand, it is a positive process of self-organisation, though somewhat contradictory. On the other hand, it provides a fertile breeding ground for extremist structures and consequently for manifestations of social terrorism that can pose a dangerous threat.

The New York Police Department analysed the way in which a person goes from ordinary life to active participation in a terrorist organisation. Following this, the future terrorist must pass through four basic stages: pre-radicalisation, self-identification, indoctrination and finally terrorisation.[1] During the first stage, a person must feel offended by a society which ignores his/her interests and the legal possibilities enabling the person to declare this must be limited. During the second stage, the offended person identifies himself/herself with a certain group to which it is possible to appeal for help with defence. During the third stage, the acquaintanceship deepens and further terrorist indoctrination occurs. Finally, during the fourth stage, active participation in a terrorist organisation begins.

According to existing estimations, members of some informal organisations are currently at the end of the second stage. An unwillingness by the establishment to take into account the interests of protest groups, brutal disregard of socially weaker groups, the inefficacy of public and state mechanisms of conflict resolution are those factors (stimuli) which will enrage future fighters of and with the system.

Another dangerous and unfortunate threat is related to an increase in radical ethno-nationalism in Ukraine, signs of which have already emerged. A good example of this is the interview with one of the leaders of the *Svoboda* party, who describes the ideology of this force.[2] Attention must also be paid to the election results of May 2008 in Kyiv. If realised, one possible consequence of this threat could be the end of democracy in Ukraine in the next few years. Therefore, we can talk about membership in NATO not as an aim of state policy but as an instrument of national security that could improve conditions for the resolution of the aforementioned problems.

Membership of NATO in a military-political union will be instrumental in enabling Ukraine to depart from its post-imperial space. In so doing it will retain the freedom to operate in the future. At the same time Ukraine's membership of the alliance can push for other democracies to hasten domestic political change. Above all, this concerns the adoption of democratic values and some kind of support for democratic society and the middle class. The first sections of Ukraine-NATO Action Plan and the annual special purpose plans

---

1 We are using a more updated scheme of radicalisation from, for example: Mitchell D. Silber and Arvin Bhatt, 'Radicalisation in the West: The Homegrown Threat', http://www.nypdshield.org/public/SiteFiles/documents/NYPD_Report_Radicalisation_in_the_West.pdf.

2 Ilyenko A., 'Natsizm – eto antipod liberal'noy tsivilizatsii', Stolichnye novosti, 29 July 2008.

are dedicated to this. They talk about political, legal and social-economic reforms.

Membership of NATO provides Ukraine with the means of strengthening its state institutions, above all, in the field of security. Strengthening of these institutions will enable the development of Ukraine substantially. According to leading experts, the development of state institutions is both urgent and a condition for the advancement of the national economy.

Membership of NATO means a fundamental increase in Ukraine's influence in a global world by enabling its participation in the mechanisms and procedures of political decisions therein.

There is, however, a problem with the terms of Euro-Atlantic integration. It is necessary to participate in the division of labour that exists in the alliance but conditions for a complete cycle of functioning of the Military Forces of Ukraine and special services should be kept. The new members of NATO were integrated and their armies built in accordance with the boutique model. This means that in place of a full-scale army, countries specialised in one area. While this is an organic approach for the Czech Republic, which specialises in chemical defence, or for Romania with its emphasis on mountain riflemen or even for the Netherlands with marines, for Ukraine, which is quite a large country, renouncing a more multifaceted approach to security may be myopic. Unlike the armed forces, the special services in NATO countries have a far smaller level of integration. At this juncture, it is important to express some thoughts on the development strategy of the domestic special services as an important instrument of defence of national interests in a modern and rapidly changing world.

Firstly, the special services do not operate in a vacuum. As a result, there cannot be any general models for construction of the secret service and counter-intelligence. In this sphere, European and Euro-Atlantic standards are non-existent. Principles by which the special services must operate in modern democratic society were developed in Europe. This concerns, in the first place, a reliable system of civil democratic control and some other aspects, which were clearly and comprehensively formulated in the recommendations of the Parliamentary Assembly of the Council of Europe 1402 (1999) and 1713 (2005). We should note, however, that in no country that was a Council of Europe member were these recommendations totally implemented.

The special services, though extraordinary, are an indispensable part of the state machinery and as such cannot be immune to its frailties. It is precisely these frailties that form the background to the present conditions and limitations on the Ukrainian special services.

Secret services and counter-intelligence can effectively operate only in close contact and with effective coordination from above. This assertion is even more accurate for Ukraine, where basic threats to national security are predominantly internal. For this reason, the system of management and coordination of activity of the special services needs to be substantially improved. This should be taken into account in the revising of the constitution. Coordination and control structures in the field of national security need to be professionalised. In particular, as noted above, the National Security and Defence Council of Ukraine have to focus on security and defence problems. Its energies should not be focused on important but less central economic aspects. Resolving this problem will facilitate more efficient democratic civil control over the activity of the special services.

Given the political instability in Ukraine, which has lasted over seven years, and the increasing politicisation of the activity of state structures, it may be useful to consider the following: that is, the possibility of creating mechanisms to coordinate the activity of the security sector organs at the executive level and in particular the Security Service of Ukraine. This will be discussed in detail in chapter 6.

The structure, forms and methods of activity of both the secret service and counter-intelligence should correspond to modern challenges and threats. V. Nalyvaychenko, acting head of the Security Service of Ukraine, notes in an article 'Adequate Response to Today's Challenges'[3] that for effective activity of the internal security service, a comprehensive solution of problems related to the defence of democracy and the state from internal and external threats is needed at the national level. Further, a clear and comprehensive definition of the place and role of the internal security service and its exceptional powers in the realisation of national security is important. Finally, an urgent task is the effective functioning of democratic civil control over the activity of counter-intelligence bodies.

Experience from the Federal Republic of Germany deserves some attention at this point. For today in modern Ukraine, as in West Germany of the 1950s–60s, there are organised groups that deny the very existence of the independent state in its present borders with support from abroad and from influential political and economic circles of the neighbouring states.

Never in history had the special services needed to protect the state, which was being destroyed by its own elite, even though they were able to stop subversive activity from outside.

The German application of the constitutional doctrine of 'armed democracy' needs to be carefully studied. This doctrine says that the state, without renouncing liberal principles, can neutralise a threat from radical and extremist groups—ideological enemies of democracy—even if the latter do not use vio-

---

3 Nalyvaychenko V., Adekvatno vidpovidaty na vyklyky syohodennya, Natsional'na bezpeka: ukrayins'kyy vymir, No. 1, 2008.

lent methods. A special strategy, with a systemic and national character following seven key directions,[4] was used for this purpose:

1. External defence of the state by the armed forces and international alliances, above all NATO;
2. The introduction of an institutional system, which ensures the balance of power, political competition, compliance of the ruling elite with general rules and the possibility of effective expression of popular will;
3. Pluralistic political process on the basis of diversity, legality of opposition, protection of minorities and liberal public opinion;
4. Political culture, which promotes tolerance, responsibility and liberalness, purposefully supported by the state;
5. Social-economic conditions supporting liberal democracy, in particular effective public policy aimed at support and strengthening of the middle class as a basic repository of democratic values in modern society;
6. Suppression of extremist political movements, which purported to come to power through violence, with repression bearing not a selective, anti-fascist or anticommunist but anti-extremist character; and
7. 'Bellicose democracy', which involves legal counteraction of the liberal state to political movements, which tried to destroy democracy by capturing state institutions through democratic procedures.

Finally, the motto 'render unto Caesar the things which are Caesar's, and unto God the things that are God's'. The police (structures of the Ministry of Internal Affairs) deal with the issues of the plunder of state property, verification of structures involved in purchases of commodities, works and services for state funds, etc. while the secret service and counter-intelligence need to support law enforcement bodies by supplying them with relevant information.

The key problem for the future of the Ukrainian Special Services is one concerning personnel. Ukraine is currently incapable of ensuring adequate social provisions (the current situation being one of personnel attrition and corruption) to nearly fifty thousand employees of organisations, which ensure state and telecommunications security as well as high profile public servants who carry out intelligence work. (In accordance with laws adopted by the Verkhovna Rada in 2005–2007, the Security Service of Ukraine comprises 33,500 people, the Department of State Protection of Ukraine 2,993, the Foreign Intelligence Service 4,350 and the Department of Special State Communications 8,250 persons). An audit on the balance of need and existing possibilities needs to be conducted. Staff numbers need reducing, remuneration needs to be set in accordance with current market standards for those who remain and adequate

---

4 Bakirov V.S., Sazonov V.I. et al. Sravnitel'naya politika. Osnovnye politicheskie sistemy sovremennogo mira, Kharkov, 2005, pp. 291–293.

social guarantees for those who are dismissed must be provided. In the process of downsising, it is crucial to assess the calibre of personnel in order to retain the most professionally qualified employees dedicated to serving the independent Ukrainian state.

It is also necessary to view both the positives and negatives in relation to the reduction of the Ukrainian army as of 2003 and in particular the granting of the right to a pension after fifteen years and the status of veteran after twenty years of service respectively.

The network of local sub-units of the Security Service of Ukraine needs to be substantially revised in terms of its efficacy, including the elimination of district, inter-district and city departments, except for a limited and clearly defined number in the most difficult regions from a security perspective, namely Crimea, Transcarpathia, Odessa, Donetsk and Bukovyna.

Demilitarisation is not a 'holy cow' but a mechanism for staffing the intelligence organs of the Security Service of Ukraine with professional and patriotic personnel as well as providing a means of democratic civil control. It is necessary to start from this point and adopt relevant decisions to facilitate this end.

The mechanisms for the provision of special services employees with medical care and housing require substantial reform. On the basis of world experience, it is necessary to define directions of such change on the basis of the famous principle 'do not harm'. Rushing the reform of present ineffective mechanisms can diminish the level of social protection, which is fairly low as it stands.

Ultimately, the problem is not the communist past—the KGB of the Ukrainian SSR died and will not resurrect, *de-KGBization* ended successfully, and in the future the state will need effective special services. The hallmark of transformation has to be assertion not denial.

Another crucial view is that Ukraine needs effective, balanced and result-oriented steps aimed at the creation of an efficient and compact intelligence community, which would defend national interests and sustain Ukraine's economic potential. It does not need reforms talks or the application of the Italian adage, so masterfully practiced in these parts, that 'everything needs to be changed in order that nothing changes'.

In achieving this purpose, it is first necessary to recognise that reform cannot be the sole responsibility of the service. Drawing from the experience of Germany, Great Britain and the USA, it is necessary to actively engage in the development of measures with both domestic and foreign experts. The leading role herein needs to be played by the Public Council of the Security Service of Ukraine and other organs of the security sector.

Secondly, the Ukrainian special services can become a dependable guarantee for the democratic advancement of Ukraine. However they also have the potential to become a danger to order in society and to the existence of the state.

Therefore, to ensure the first modification, it is necessary to make a lot of effort; for the second, there is no need to do anything in particular. It is not sufficient to leave everything as it is and time is of the essence.

On the whole, it is possible to say that what is needed to be done is obvious. There are people who can do it but resolve and steadfast political will are needed.

Finally, we would like to quote one of the leading statesmen of the Ukrainian state in the stormy 1917–1921 years, S. Petlyura:

> *Tasks that are included in the jurisdiction of intelligence and counterintelligence activity of the Council need to be specified. New spotless and state traditions of this service need to be introduced... It is necessary to form the core of state-minded and intelligent officers who would create new directions in this sphere. I think that it is possible to achieve this not only through selection of the personnel, but also through creation of the necessary literature and courses. Here, in my opinion, it is necessary to achieve the neutralisation of that harmful and even criminal prejudice, which was and remains characteristic of our army (especially the officers) and our citizenship in relation to the mentioned service. Possibly the prejudice has an explanation, but in essence it is imprudent and in terms of consequences even criminal, because it is clear that without a well functioning service our state authorities will fail... It is necessary that citizens know the positive role of this service and support its work with sympathy and help.*

Briefly, we would like to discuss three alternatives to the policy of Euro-Atlantic integration. First is an actively discussed *European security policy*. A principal technical advantage of the alliance is the presence of coordinated C3I systems (command, control, communications and intelligence), which are the bases of modern warfare. There are no European powers with such an efficient system but it does not mean they do not plan to create something similar.

The European security policy is created not as an alternative to NATO but as an organic addition to the capacities and potential of the alliance aimed to guarantee security by non-military means and counteract new challenges, including organised crime, illegal migration, proliferation of weapons of mass destruction, illegal drugs trafficking and migration, etc.

As noted by H. Yavors'ka, the basic EU document adopted in place of the constitution—the Treaty of Lisbon—directly refers to the North Atlantic Treaty Organisation in the part about solidarity and responsibility in relation to mutual protection of EU countries from military aggression, terrorist attack, natural or manmade catastrophes. Namely, '...responsibilities and collaboration of countries – EU members in the security and defence sphere must correspond to responsibilities within NATO, which for those countries which are its members remain the basis of their collective defence'.

As stated by the French Minister of Defence Hervé Morin at the 44th Munich Security Conference in February 2008, 'The European Union and NATO are needed and complementary... NATO and EU are for us the two constituent parts of one policy of security and defence'. The minister of defence of Germany, Franz Jozef Jung, noted that 'NATO-EU cooperation is needed more than ever on the scenes of today's operations'.

The planning of security of and in the EU, aimed at the development of police, gendarme forces, forces for post-conflict reconstruction, etc., is based on an understanding of the European security policy as complementary to NATO.

The second direction is membership of the Collective Security Treaty Organisation (CSTO). It is a union with absolute dominance by the Russian Federation and is a generally weaker organisation politically, economically and militarily. It is a return to the place from which Ukraine departed seventeen years ago. No less important is that its response is based on very different values. Becoming party to such a collective would involve taking on an additional load of Russian problems, which together with domestic ones would almost surely destroy Ukraine's independence.

The Shanghai Cooperation Organisation (SCO), actively advertised in Ukraine, can also be considered in the same category. The organisation was created in 2001 by the People's Republic of China, the Russian Federation, Kazakhstan, Uzbekistan, Tajikistan and Kyrgyzstan for the development of collaboration and counteraction of extremism, terrorism and separatism in the region. Observers of the organisation are India, Pakistan, Iran and Byelorussia. The territory of the SCO states exceeds one fourth of the total earth's surface and collectively they have enormous economic potential.

The organisation has a pronounced regional (Eurasian) character. S. Ivanov, former minister of defence of the Russian Federation, expressed doubt about the possibility of Byelorussia's full membership of SCO on the basis that it had an exceptionally European character. It should be remembered that all SCO states have authoritarian regimes.

Furthermore, the August 2008 events in Georgia proved a rather virtual character of CSTO in a critical situation. CSTO did not play any role and was not even able to produce a statement. However, in the opinion of the Russian political scientist A. Piontkovskiy, CSTO actually serves as an instrument for Beijing's penetration into Central Asia, which became evident again in the organisation's Dushanbe Declaration. This is not surprising given that the Gross Domestic Product of the People's Republic of China's economy is almost three times more that of other SCO countries with a population of six times more.

The third alternative, over which there is much lively discussion, is neutrality. According to the Ukrainian researcher O. Bohomolov, Ukraine is already a neutral and non-aligned state. As a result, its bright neutral future can be observed in the here and now. And there are no reasons to hope for anything other than the present indefinite state.

British experts note that it is impossible to talk about uncertainty, in the event Ukraine acquires the legal status of neutrality, of further participation of the state in joint NATO and EU security and defence programs.

Some politicians see in neutrality a prototype of national idea, a uniting core. Five European countries, in accordance with international traditions, are recognised as being neutral: Austria, Ireland, Finland, Sweden and Switzerland. All of them observe neutrality, although in legal terms this status translates differently in every country.

These five countries are members of the UN and OSCE, and cooperate with NATO in the framework of the program 'Partnership for Peace'. Except for Switzerland, all are members of the EU and even take part in the rapid reaction force of the EU yet none of them has foreign bases on its territory.

When comparing the defence capabilities of these countries with Ukraine, the picture is as follows. In all neutral countries the economy is highly developed and stable, with levels of GDP exceeding that of Ukraine's between three and five times and GDP per capita between twenty to thirty-five times greater. Neutral countries have a high level of military expenditure, exceeding that of Ukraine by four and a half to twelve times. They also possess large armed forces and developed defence industries.

These features enable these countries to carry out a main function that stems from their neutrality—to defend themselves with their own forces and resources without participating in the systems of collective defence. Lately, however, other views have been spreading rapidly in Sweden and Finland.

Each neutral country has its own model and history of neutrality. They often talk about Switzerland but Ukraine is not Switzerland. Not because it is not located in a mountain region but because it does not have the same resources, namely a reliable banking system that would serve both the interests of any opposing sides.

Both the Russian Federation and NATO countries are interested in the resources of Ukraine. We should mention not Switzerland but Belgium and the Netherlands, whose internationally recognised neutrality could not prevent aggression during world wars.

The neutrality of Austria after the Second World War was governed by 'the German question'. As has already been mentioned, the creation of NATO had three aims: to keep the USA in Europe, Russia out of Europe and

Germany under control. Austria's membership of NATO would strengthen Germany, which was a perceived danger. After two communist *putsches* in 1955, a state agreement that confirmed Austria's neutrality was signed.

Finland's neutrality was ensured in a difficult defence during the 'Winter War' in 1940, which began at once after Helsinki signed the convention of the League of Nations about absolute neutrality. The leadership of the USSR realised that the cost of Finland's annexation would exceed all possible spoils. For this reason, during the 1950s–1980s, the Kremlin carried out the policy of Finlandisation, using the Scandinavian country as a bridge between blocs.

While discussing the question of armed neutrality for Ukraine, its material-financial aspect should not be ignored. According to preliminary estimates, it would involve an army amounting to one percent of the population equipped with modern armaments. We should also remember the necessity to form a powerful system of the special services and police, which would stall an encircling siege in response to potential regional problems.

The problem of neutrality is often mentioned in relation to the Budapest Memorandum of 1994. It concerns security guarantees in relation to Ukraine's accession to the Treaty on the Non-Proliferation of Nuclear Weapons on December 5th 1994. Together with notes from France and the People's Republic of China, the UN Charter, the final act of the CSCE, documents which accompanied the disintegration of the USSR, and a system of agreements about friendship and good neighbourly relations, it forms the basis of the system of international guarantees of independence, sovereignty and the territorial integrity of Ukraine.

Out of six articles of the memorandum, two refer to the Helsinki Act, two to the UN Charter and yet another two to the Treaty on the Non-Proliferation of Nuclear Weapons. Only one, the sixth article, does not contain any references. However, it guarantees a conduct of consultations among the states-guarantors on the case of emerging situations and the question about responsibilities. Thus to answer a question about the feasibility of the Budapest guarantees, it is necessary to refer to other abovementioned documents.

Concerning Article 2, the last sixty-three years have shown too many examples of the skilful evasion of the stipulations of the UN Charter and an open neglect of its spirit. Ultimately it is possible to question the existing borders without the use of force. Anyone with matter-of-fact views, however, would believe in a full-scale armed invasion against Ukraine, while intelligence-subversive activity against our state, in some regions, is a proven fact.

Article 3 contains economic guarantees. The winter of 2005–2006 and the 'Gazprom' threats are memorable. Economic pressure was asserted by one of the guarantors and how the mechanisms of the memorandum worked then is not worthy of mention. The relevant stipulations of the 'Big Agreement' of 1997 turned out to be that 'effective'. The phrase of Napoleon 'the truth is usually on the side of the big battalions', with the necessary corrections, was confirmed at a later time.

Ukraine can only assist itself. The only reliable guarantees can be a prosperous economy, developed civil society with strong state institutions and above all the army, secret services and diplomatic service.

Let us return to the most pressing question—the Membership Action Plan (MAP). Fortunately for some and unfortunately for others it is necessary to be mindful that the NATO Membership Action Plan is above all a program of internal reforms. It is not even a promise of accession. Undoubtedly, it is a powerful mechanism of control for overseeing effective change in the army and special services. After the implementation of MAP, which differs only in its mechanisms for control from the present special purpose Ukraine-NATO plan, Ukraine will have a more effective system of controlling national security. Consequently, this will strengthen Ukraine's potential to defend its independence, sovereignty and territorial integrity. For this reason, it is impossible not to support the experts, who argue in favour of the necessity of practical reform measures, without regard to the availability or absence of the declared international programs.

Further, the basis of MAP, like other special purpose plans and national programs of actions, is in no way security and defence reform but one of political, economic and legal transformation. Nobody is more interested than Ukraine in the realisation of these changes.

There is one further matter. Success of reforms in young democracies is, in great measure, determined by lessons from international experience. Otherwise, it 'Does not matter which party we build, we end up with the Communist Party of the Soviet Union'. There are problems however. How many millions have international consultants plundered? Therefore it is crucial to draw on professionals from reputable organisations that are accountable to their government.

Finally, NATO is not the answer. Membership in the alliance will only create a field of positive opportunities, which should be used by Ukraine. Experience of cooperation with the alliance, acquired during the review of defence and the security sector as well as during the execution of special purpose Ukraine-NATO plans, proves convincingly that advantage can be taken of this opportunity to accelerate reforms and guarantee the democratic advancement of society.

Developing a Strategic Planning and Security Sector Management System: An Urgent National Security Task

The focus of analysis in this chapter will be problems related to the establishment and development of the Ukrainian security sector, above all the systems for its strategic management. According to a generally accepted definition, the security sector consists of the higher bodies of management, the armed forces, uniformed or civil police, the gendarmerie, the intelligence services, border control, the internal security services and militia and other armed formations that work for the country or are associated with it. In other words, the executive level of the security sector includes the intelligence and internal security services, the police, border control and defence forces.[1]

But why do we talk of a strategic level of management of the national security sector? The main reason is that today national security has become perhaps the most important factor in national-state identity and in the geopolitical orientation and consolidation of society in Ukraine in an often contradictory and fast-changing modern world. At the same time, experience in the development of independent statehood, above all over the last decade, confirms that the strategic level remains the weakest and most vulnerable when it comes to external influences in the current Ukrainian management system of the national security sector.

In recent years, interested members of the public and experts in Ukraine, European states, the USA and Canada had the opportunity to familiarise themselves thoroughly with the Ukrainian security sector and the features of its functioning. This became possible due to the development of collaboration between Ukraine and NATO, in particular within the framework of a NATO-Ukraine Joint High Level Working Group on Defence Reform (JWGDR) with active participation of the Ukrainian research centres and our foreign colleagues, and above all the Geneva Centre for the Democratic Control of Armed Forces (DCAF).

We would like to provide one example. At the beginning of 2006 an important piece of work, an English-language collection (over 900 pages) of acts of Ukrainian legislation in the field of national security and defence with

1 Resolution of the Parliamentary Assembly of the Council of Europe 1713 (2005).

commentaries, was published. Experts at the top level of the International Secretariat of NATO, the Secretariat of the National Security and Defence Council of Ukraine as well as the Secretariat of the Verkhovna Rada of Ukraine and the Geneva Centre for the Democratic Control of Armed Forces worked on it. This publication provides a fairly complete picture of the features of the Ukrainian security sector: its constituent parts, its working principles and management mechanisms and the democratic control over the activities of the structures and departments of the security sector.[2]

As has already been highlighted, between 1996 and 1997, a system of strategic management for the security sector of Ukraine in its present shape was formed and a number of key issues related to national security policy were successfully resolved. In particular, in 1997 the Verkhovna Rada adopted the 'Concept of National Security', which defined the vitally important national aims of Ukraine and the ways to realise them. The state borders of Ukraine became internationally recognised and guaranteed through the signature of international agreements with neighbouring states and the adoption of the 'Charter for a Distinctive Ukraine-NATO Partnership' defined in broad terms the Euro-Atlantic course for Kyiv.

The strategic level of management of national security generally and the security sector as its key constituent part in particular have not, on the whole, experienced substantial changes since then notwithstanding substantial changes in the security situation and in the configuration of state power following the constitutional reform in 2004 and the reform of the security sector bodies between 2004 and 2007.

At present, the state constituent parts of the security sector of Ukraine include the strategic management and executive levels. Therefore, the strategic management level is represented by the Verkhovna Rada, the president, the National Security and Defence Council and the Cabinet of Ministers whilst the executive level is made up of the defence agencies, namely: the Armed forces, the State Special Transport Service, the military sub-units of the Ministry of Emergency Situations and Protection of the Population (a result of the Chernobyl catastrophe), the State Service for Special Communications and Protection of Information, the internal Security Service, the intelligence services (the Foreign Intelligence Service, the Chief Intelligence Directorate of the Ministry of Defence, the Intelligence Directorate of the Administration of the State Border Service), the police (the Ministry of Internal Affairs), the internal troops of the Ministry of Internal Affairs (gendarmerie), the Directorate of State Protection and border control (the State Border Service). The State Department for the Execution of Sentences to some extent also belongs to the security sector.

---

2 Colston J., Fluri P., Piroshkov S. (eds.), The Security Sector Legislation of Ukraine, 2006.

According to Article 85 of the constitution, the plenary powers of the Verkhovna Rada include the determination of the principles of internal and external policy, the making of a public announcement upon a declaration by the president of Ukraine of a state of war and the signature of peace treaties. They also include approval of the president's decisions relating to the use of the Armed Forces and other military formations in the case of aggression against Ukraine; approval of the President's decrees in relation to a state of war or emergency situations; mobilisation of forces and the declaration of a region or regions as an area or areas of natural emergency or disaster. It should be noted separately that the Verkhovna Rada has the right to carry out parliamentary control within limits defined within the constitution (Article 85). This is explicitly laid out in Article 92 which deals with: principles of external relations, foreign economic activity and customs; bases of national security, organisation of the Armed forces of Ukraine and provision of public order; the legal regime of the state border, state of war or emergency situations and areas of natural emergency or disaster. The same article also explicitly sets out the procedures for sending sub-units of the Armed Forces to other states as well as the procedures for deployment of foreign troops within Ukrainian territory.

Parliament, in accordance with Article 89 of the constitution, has set up the Committee on National Security and Defence. Within its structure, this committee has six sub-committees dealing with, amongst other things, military security and defence as well as state security. This committee has fairly extensive powers, some of which have been invoked especially over the last few years.

The president of Ukraine, in accordance with Basic Law (Article 106), exercises general control in the spheres of national security and defence of the state. His remit is to ensure state independence, national security and the legal succession of the state. He also represents the state in international relations, manages foreign policy, including making decisions about the recognition of foreign states and the exchange of diplomatic representatives, and controls the announcement of martial law, the partial or general mobilisation of the forces and manages emergency situations as well as areas of natural emergency or disaster. In accordance with Article 106 of the constitution, the president of Ukraine has the right of appointment and dismissal of the higher command of the Armed Forces and other military formations. In summary, therefore, it should be emphasised that the head of state exercises control in the sphere of national security and defence and chairs the National Security and Defence Council of Ukraine (NSDCU).

The fulfilment of these functions is realised with the help of the National Security and Defence Council of Ukraine. This constitutional body organises and controls the activities of the organs of executive power in the areas of national security and defence along with the help of auxiliary consultative bodies, of which the main one is the Secretariat of the President of Ukraine.

The NSDCU derives its status as a coordinating body accountable to the president of Ukraine from Article 107 of the constitution. This article also governs its function of coordinating and controlling the activities of the organs of executive power in the field of national security and defence and determines in part the committee's composition (prime minister, minister of defence, chairman of the Security Service, minister for internal affairs and minister for foreign affairs). It also provides for the implementation of decisions taken through decrees of the president of Ukraine. The article furthermore stipulates that the chairman of the Verkhovna Rada can attend and take part in meetings of the NSDCU providing some parliamentary control in the area of national security and defence.

In accordance with Article 3 of the Law of Ukraine, 'On the National Security and Defence Council of Ukraine', the functions of the council are stated to include the following:

1. Submitting proposals to the president on the implementation of the fundamentals of domestic and foreign policy in the sphere of national security and defence;
2. Coordinating and controlling the activities of the organs of executive power in the sphere of national security and defence during peacetime; and
3. Coordinating and controlling the activities of the organs of executive power in the sphere of national security and defence during the imposition of martial law or in a state of emergency or during other crises that threaten the national security of Ukraine.

In accordance with Article 14 of the Law of Ukraine, 'On the National Security and Defence Council of Ukraine', working and advisory organs can be created by decision of the council.

The same article provides that the supply of information to and analytical and organisational support for the activity of the NSDCU is given by its secretariat, which presently includes departments of military and state security.

Based within the NSDCU is the National Institute for Problems of International Security, the Institute for Problems of National Security and the Interdepartmental Centre for the Fight against Organised Crime, all of which carry out research and provide information to and analytic support for the council.

The Chief Service for Security and Defence Policy operates within the Secretariat of the President of Ukraine. The National Institute of Strategic

Studies and the National Specialised Centre for Euro-Atlantic Integration also report to the president of Ukraine.

During the presidential term of V. Yushchenko, there was no clear delineation of power between the Secretariat of the President of Ukraine and the NSDCU. However, explicit powers of the secretariat included the day-to-day support for the activities of the head of state, including personnel policy support in the security sector bodies.

The Cabinet of Ministers is the highest organ in the system of executive authorities in Ukraine. In accordance with Article 116 of the constitution, it has responsibility for the implementation of foreign policy and external economic activity and, in the field of customs, implements measures for ensuring defence capability and national security. In addition, it is responsible for protecting Ukrainian interests, ensuring legality in state affairs, protecting the rights and freedoms and property of its citizens, ensuring public order and fighting crime. The government of Ukraine prepares the state budget and provides financial as well as material-technical support to the security sector. Following the constitutional reform of 2004, the cabinet ministers direct and coordinate the work of the ministries and other organs of executive power. They also appoint a number of important state officials.

In accordance with Article 19 of the Law of Ukraine, 'On the Cabinet of Ministers of Ukraine', the government is responsible for national security and defence capability and, in accordance with Article 20, the Cabinet of Ministers:

- Implements measures related to the defence of the state border of Ukraine and its territories;
- Implements measures for the strengthening of national security, and develops and adopts state programs in relation thereto;
- Implements measures for the improvement of military efficiency of the armed forces and determines, within the budgetary allocations for defence, the number of Ukrainian citizens liable for conscription to regular military service and training;
- Implements measures for the provision of defence capability and the equipping of the armed forces and other military bodies formed in accordance with the law;
- Provides social and legal guarantees to servicemen, persons exempt from military service and to members of their families;
- Decides on participation of servicemen of Ukraine in peacekeeping operations in accordance with the procedure determined in the law; and
- Ensures financial and material-technical support for the activities of law enforcement authorities, as well as social protection of their employees and members of their families.

In accordance with Article 50 of the same law, the activities of government as a collective body are supported by the Secretariat of the Cabinet of Ministers of Ukraine. The directorate for the activities of justice and law enforcement authorities (whose head is ex officio a deputy minister of the Cabinet of Ministers) and the directorate for questions of defence and mobilisation are part of the secretariat.

Section VII of the law regulates the relationships between the Cabinet of Ministers and the president of Ukraine, the NSDCU and the advisory bodies to the head of state. The government is required to ensure the implementation of acts of the president, provide him/her with the necessary information, and cabinet ministers can take part in the operation of the working bodies of the head of state.

In summary, the Verkhovna Rada determines the basic principles of public policy in the field of national security; the president of Ukraine through the National Security and Defence Council of Ukraine directly defines the strategic and doctrine elements of this policy and implements the staffing policy; and the government directly implements the policy, in particular ensuring financial and social protection of servicemen and employees of law enforcement authorities. This distribution of power relates primarily to peacetime.

Under conditions of martial law, in accordance with the Law 'On the defence of Ukraine', General Headquarters of the Supreme High Command headed by the head of state are created for the management of the defence of Ukraine against aggression.

The management system described above for the bodies making up the security sector has, over a period of almost two years, proven its general capacity to carry out difficult complex tasks related to the management of national security. In particular, a number of steps have been taken towards democratisation of the security sector and the strengthening of democratic civil control over the activities of its constituent bodies.

During this time, the first complex review of the security sector in the history of an independent Ukraine was conducted, the results of which were reflected in the adoption by the president of Ukraine in January 2007 of the National Security Strategy of Ukraine, the Concept of Reform of Criminal Justice (April 2008), the Concept of Reform of the Security Service of Ukraine (March 2008), the Concept of Reform of the State Border Service (July 2007), several decisions of the NSDCU, and 'White Books' of the security sector organs of Ukraine in 2007. A number of other questions of strategic importance were resolved.

However, over time, a number of problems have emerged. The basic problems are as follows.

The first is having the security sector organs answerable to both the president and the Cabinet of Ministers, a symptom of the general imperfection and imbalance of the Ukrainian system of state power. The great majority of these 'organs' (with the exception of the internal security service of the Security Service of Ukraine and the intelligence services—especially the Foreign Intelligence Service) are organs of executive power and their activities are, accordingly, directed by the Cabinet of Ministers. At the same time, as has been noted already, general management in the field of national security and defence is carried out by the head of state.

Perhaps this contradiction is most explicitly expressed in the Law 'On the State Service of Special Communications and Protection of Information'. Article 2 asserts that the State Service of Special Communications and Protection of Information is directed by the Cabinet of Ministers. At the same time, however, in questions of defence the same body reports to the president. It should be borne in mind that the function of the service mainly relates to the protection of national security but the head of state does not have real influence within its structure.

The contradiction is less evident but no less problematic where the Security Service and intelligence organs are concerned. These are not organs of executive power but a substantial part of their activity directly concerns questions of executive power.

Such a lack of clear delineation with, in some cases, direct overlap of powers, can result in difficult and insoluble contradictions even in more stable political situations with longer political traditions than presently exist in Ukraine. These problems substantially worsen during periods of so-called 'cohabitation' when the president and the government belong to different political forces. The dangerous effects of such a situation became apparent in the summer of 2007 when opposing views among sub-units of different security sector bodies became obvious, namely between the Ministry for Internal Affairs and the Directorate of State Protection.

It should also be remembered that there is a high turnover in the personnel of the higher state authorities. In particular, a changeover in personnel of seven secretaries within the National Security and Defence Council has occurred in the last four years alone. In the main, this can be explained by a fast changing political situation. However, it does significantly complicate the decision-making process in routine current questions related to the management of national security.

Less obvious but potentially just as difficult is the problem of the lack of delineation between the political and administrative management of the security sector. The practice of appointing political figures as heads of law enforcement authorities and special services, widely exercised after the constitutional reform of 2004, can be problematic in the absence of properly defined procedures enshrined in law for separately addressing political and professional questions. The most important among such problems is the threat of the politicisation of the activities of the security sector and making them subordinate to political forces to the detriment of national interests.

There are also other issues that are less a matter of principle. The ultimate resolution of such problems is possible only within the framework of the planned state constitutional and administrative reforms, the necessity of which all leading political forces in Ukraine agree upon.

At the same time, it is possible to change the present situation through the introduction within the sector of a security model, which has already functioned successfully over a period of 15 years in the resolution of military security issues.

The essence of this model is contained within Article 11 of the Law 'On the Defence of Ukraine' which states that 'the General Staff of the Armed Forces comprise the principal military body responsible for defence planning, directing the deployment of the Armed Forces, and coordinating control over the execution of state defence tasks through the executive, local self-government organs, other state military organisations and law-enforcement organs created in accordance with the laws of Ukraine. These aforementioned state organs operate within predetermined legal limits recited within this law and other laws as well as by the normative-legal acts of the President of Ukraine, the Verkhovna Rada of Ukraine and the Cabinet of Ministers of Ukraine'.

Thus, the present day-to-day management issues of military security are dealt with by the General Staff of the armed forces whose leadership is not political and is far more stable and professional.

For this reason, the president of Ukraine determined in the Concept of Reform of the Security Service of Ukraine (adopted in March 2008) that among the basic functions of the Security Service of Ukraine that need to be reflected in the new version of the Law of Ukraine 'On the Security Service of Ukraine', all in accordance with the legislative regulation and practice of internal security organisations of the European states, 'coordination, within the limits of jurisdiction determined in the legislation, of measures related to the provision of the national security of Ukraine in the area of state security'. This decision of the head of state mainly arises from the fact that in accordance with the Law of Ukraine 'On the Bases of National Security of Ukraine' and the National Security Strategy of Ukraine, the key threats to national security are internal or come about through internal factors.

Enshrining in legislation clear lines of responsibility for the coordination of state security to the Security Service of Ukraine and the creation of clear and effective procedures for its implementation will help substantially to promote efficient functioning of the security sector and, above all, of the internal security and intelligence services where it comes to the mitigation and neutralisation of actual and potential threats to national security.

Also, it should be noted that the constitution and current legislation assume a developed system of democratic civil control over the activities of the Security Service. In particular, a special position of 'Representative of the President of Ukraine on control over the activity of the Security Service of Ukraine' was created, which is a unique position within the state authority system in Ukraine. Furthermore, the chairman of the Ukrainian internal security service, unique among the leaders of the security sector organs, is proposed by the head of state and approved by parliament.

Conclusions

The tasks on the Ukrainian agenda can be logically divided into several key groups. First of all, it is necessary to determine the ideological basis for action. The present ideological chaos, resulting from liberals and authoritarian traditionalists coming together in their fervent common recognition of a Ukrainian state, worked on the whole during the protracted fight for independence. 'The Orange Revolution' has finally ended this post-Soviet stage in Ukrainian history and has opened up the possibility for clear formulation of different positions without fear of causing damage to the state. This, without doubt, does not concern military operations. On the contrary, this kind of certainty will help in the understanding of what possibilities and potential unions exist. It is time to define both clearly and critically what is most important: namely, the choice between human rights and a European Ukraine on the one hand and a ghostly bygone national grandeur fighting against its very real enemies on the other. The state must serve the person and society and not vice versa.

Such differentiation will allow the resolution of a number of very important problems. It will allow a distinction to be made between ethnic and civil nationalism, which comes close to xenophobia and is inclined to resolve all problems by so-called 'simple and reliable' authoritarian means.

We need to proclaim the dominant influence of a clerical ideology in public life, of the civil character of our state and that superstition and paganism of a most primitive type amounts to public religion.

We need to end the eternal fighting—fighting for what and with whom has become unclear. We need finally to climb out from the trenches and carry out the orders of Grebenschikov's 'Colonel Vasin' because new intelligence information from the secret services about the war with us is being confirmed on a daily basis for the 20 years that have passed since this song was written. If Petro Hryhorenko wrote that only rats live underground, we are convinced that epic heroes live mainly in trenches.

At present, since the August 2008 events in Georgia, we should add that all of us are 'in the same boat'. It is necessary to understand that the personal future of the ruling groups depends on the survival of the country.

Finally, we would like to express openly what exactly it is that we dislike about modern Russia. Unlike traditionalists, our phobia is not rooted in racial differences (the Finno-Ugrians created the most pleasant lifestyle in the Baltic states), not in history (it is not only the Great Russians that have terrible pages in their history book, all peoples do, including the Ukrainians) and not even in their offensives (after all the Poles, the Turks and the Germans have all caused quite a bit of suffering to us but we have done the same to them). Rather, it lies in an authoritarian, anachronistic state, in abysmally backward public institutions and in national aspirations that are a century out of date. In summary, Russia is disliked because it repeats its history, turning this, undoubtedly, great country into the biggest threat to itself and its neighbours. Furthermore, the thoughts of Petr Chaadaev on this subject have already been known for two hundred years.

Second, quality discussions on current public issues are needed. The mass media need to formulate their agenda. We need to be more active in producing materials setting out a programme that is rich in content rather than short-lived propaganda or leaflets to stir the masses. Without doubt, 'stirring up' and propaganda are important but good material needs to be widely distributed and explained. In Ukraine, there is no serious intellectual liberal base for the wide circles of people who think about or even aim to do this.

As a result, even although the task is clearly and simply formulated, it is difficult to execute. The basic real problems for modern Ukrainian society need to be defined; the important questions raised and concrete answers need to be given to them. We need not only to write and talk but also to act.

In pragmatic terms, however, we must not rush this. On the contrary, we need to give real meaning to the Euro-Atlantic course and consequently fulfil the special purpose plan—the national program—and carry out real reforms in the security and defence sectors. The NATO 'umbrella' is necessary more than ever when the first gusts of the future storm can already be perceived. It does not provide absolute guarantees but will give certain freedom of action in the future and confidence through support.

It is necessary to develop relations with the USA as well as with neighbouring countries and members of the alliance. We need to work in Berlin and Paris and persuade them of the benefits of a relationship with Ukraine. We need to get the support of the European elite: perhaps the most positive moment in the lead-up to the Bucharest summit was the statement of the French philosopher André Glucksmann about unreserved support for the Euro-Atlantic aspirations of Ukraine.

One important strategy is the development of relationships with neighbours. We need strategic relationships with Warsaw, Vilnius, Riga and Tallinn, and friendly and close relations with Slovakia, Czech Republic and Hungary. A separate strategy relates to Turkey. Persistent work based on the agreement of non-controversial interests and economic collaboration has a potential to take relations to a new level. In cooperation with Bucharest, it is necessary to emphasise our common interests rather than areas of dispute arising from toughly protecting our own national interests.

And, finally, we must remember the Kremlin. We must work with Russia. It does not take much to irritate Moscow. A tough but clear, transparent and predictable line is needed. A cordial approach to our relations is needed. And in saying this, we are talking not only about gas.

We must develop a policy and action plan at the highest state level for the withdrawal of the Russian Federation's Black Sea Fleet from Ukrainian territory and be focussed and persistent in its implementation. We are already at a stage when we need to discuss with the Russians the question of their withdrawal and the transfer of facilities. We need to keep a watch on their activities in the construction of a military naval base in Novorossiysk and actively involve the relevant capabilities of the USA and EU for this purpose.

By maintaining a stance on the main issues, concessions can be made on less important questions. We should not waste time on small or emotive issues that will only serve to irritate the other side. The need to provide positive TV footage to Moscow should also not be forgotten.

The campaign for the dissemination of information explaining Ukraine's stance both to its own population and to the world must become a priority. In general, it is clear what needs to be done and the strengths and weaknesses of the other side are also known. It should be stated again that it is persistence and strong political determination that are needed. Indeed, it is this that marks the character of a true statesman.

It is also essential that Ukraine's position be both clear and balanced. Russia was and will continue to be our largest neighbour, a strategic partner both in our country's economy and culturally. The history of our bilateral relations calls to mind a quotation from Antoine de Saint-Exupéry's 'The Little Prince': 'One becomes responsible, forever, for that which one has tamed'. The influence of our country on the establishment and development of the Russian Empire, of which the modern Russian Federation considers itself the successor, can hardly be overestimated. Ukrainians, and in particular the professors of the Kyiv-Mohyla Academy, developed the ideological basis for this power in the 17th century. For this reason, the great Frenchman's writing can be taken further: the courteous but firm stand taken by Ukraine will help Russia to overcome its problems and take her proper place as one of Europe's great countries.

The most important issue before us is that of the systematic reform of Ukraine. A democratic state that ensures the supremacy of law must be developed. Money cannot replace the courts. We need to realise that glamour cannot take the place of professionalism. There needs to be extended access to the middle classes to decision making and childish games need to stop—everybody must be responsible for their own words and deeds.

All this affects the administration including territorial administration, judicial reform and reform of the criminal justice system. A major transformation is needed in the economy, in the development of an efficient land market, expedient deregulation, as well as a tranche of liberal social-economic reforms in the areas of pension, housing, healthcare, social security, etc.

Ukraine needs a strong security sector. The Georgia example has shown that having a strong army and special services is not sufficient, but that not having them is a guarantee for loss of independence. Quick and decisive reforms are needed. The state must engage both new and old skilled and democratically minded professionals in the management of the security sector, especially in the army, the organisations responsible for security, the internal troops and the police.

If there is no effective state, GDP percentages and standard of living data will not help. One need only look to the former 'Switzerland of the Near East', the name by which, until 1974, Lebanon was known. But then followed decades of civil war provoked by the diversity of its society together with a weak and inefficient state.

It must be repeated, however, that all that has been said above is not intended in any way to be regarded as advice to political leaders. The authors are neither that presumptuous nor that vain. That said, they are convinced that it is only possible to guarantee the security of Ukraine by changing it and all the possibilities for doing this lie within our hands.

Finally, we would like to endorse the words of the secretary of the National Security and Defence Council of Ukraine, R. Bohatyrev, when he said that 'Ukraine is facing a number of very serious challenges and problems, which need urgent solutions. But every threat has a potential for subsequent development. The bigger the threat, the more potential there is. Therefore, we need to seize the opportunities. It is time to unite all the intellectual resources of our country. We have had enough of feudal wars and medieval break-ups. It is time to rise from the ashes'.

List of Contributors

Volodymyr P. Horbulin

V. Horbulin—head of the Council for Foreign and Security Policy, politician, doctor of engineering, professor, member of the National Academy of Sciences of Ukraine and director of the Institute of National Security Problems at the National Security and Defence Council of Ukraine—was born on 17 January 1939 in Zaporizhzhya city.

In 1962, he graduated from the Physico-technical Faculty of Dnipropetrovsk University and received a mechanical engineer's diploma ("flying crafts"). In 1994, V. Horbulin received his doctorate in Engineering Science. He became a professor in 2005 and a member of the National Academy of Sciences of Ukraine in 1997.

In the years 1962 to 1977, V. Horbulin worked at "Pivdenne" design office (Dnipropetrovsk city) and participated in the development of the strategic rocket systems and space vehicles of the "Kosmos" series. From 1977 to 1990, he worked at the Central Committee of the Communist Party of Ukraine and in 1980 he headed the sector of the rocket and aircraft technologies. He participated in the organisation and coordination of all programme activities concerning the establishment of rocket, space and aircraft equipment in Ukraine.

In 1990, he was appointed head of the Subdivision of Defence Complex, Communications and Machine Building of the Cabinet of Ministers of Ukraine. In 1992, he became the general director of the National Space Agency of Ukraine. He managed its development and directly participated in the implementation of the first National Space Programme of Ukraine (1992–1994). Mr. Horbulin is a member of the International Academy of Astronautics.

In August 1994, V. Horbulin was appointed secretary of the Council of National Security under the president of Ukraine; in October 1994, he became adviser to the president of Ukraine for national security issues. From August 1996 to November 1999, he was the secretary of the Council of National Security and Defence of Ukraine. V. Horbulin is the co-author of the Concept of National Security and Defence of Ukraine, the State Programme of Building and Development of Armed Forces of Ukraine, and other key documents of state building and development.

From July 2000 to December 2002, he held the position of head of the State Commission for the Military-Industrial Complex of Ukraine. He managed and took part in the development of the State Programme of Armament and

Military Equipment Development and the Concept of Structural Reorganisation of the Military-Industrial Complex of Ukraine. In December 2002, he was appointed assistant to the president of Ukraine for national security issues.

Following the order of the president of Ukraine (January 2003), he established the National Centre of Euro-Atlantic Integration of Ukraine headed by him pro bono.

From March 2003 to January 2005, he was the deputy head of the State Commission for Reformation and Development of Armed Forces of Ukraine. He participated directly in the development of the Strategic Defence Bulletin of Ukraine for the period to 2015, the Military Doctrine of Ukraine (June 2004) and the Law "On Fundamentals of National Security of Ukraine" (June 2003).

In December 2003, V. Horbulin became the organiser and director of the Institute of National Security Problems of Ukraine. In 2005, he was appointed the adviser to the president of Ukraine and acting head of the Principal Service of Defence Policy at the Secretariat of the President of Ukraine. In May 2006, V. Horbulin was appointed acting secretary of the Council of National Security and Defence of Ukraine. He headed and participated in the development of the Strategy of National Security of Ukraine. Mr. Horbulin took part in the development of the Concept of Reformation of the Security Service of Ukraine and the White Book "The Security Service and Intelligence Agencies of Ukraine."

In November 2007, he obtained the position of director of the Institute of National Security Problems and became the editor-in-chief of *Ecology and Resources* magazine.

In November 2000, V. Horbulin became a member of the Presidium of the Committee of State Prizes of Ukraine in Science and Technology.

Before November 1999, he headed the State Interagency Commission for Cooperation with NATO and co-headed the Consulting Committee under the presidents of Ukraine and Poland, co-headed the Secretariat of Kuchma-Gore Commission. From 2000 to 2001, V. Horbulin headed the Interagency Commission for Political Conflict Resolution in the Transdniestria region of the Republic of Moldova. From November 2000 to December 2002, he was the deputy head of the Governmental Committee for Defence, Military-Industrial Complex and Law Enforcement.

Volodymyr Horbulin was the first editor-in-chief of the *Strategic Panorama* scientific and practical magazine.

V. Horbulin is the laureate of the State Prize in Science and Technology (2002), laureate of the USSR Prize in Science and Technology (1990), laureate of M. K. Yangel State Prize of the National Academy of Sciences of Ukraine (1988). Volodymyr Horbulin was awarded Orders of the Red Banner of Labour (1976 and 1982), the Order of Prince Yaroslav the Wise of the 5th grade (April 1997) and 4th grade (January 2004), and medals. V. Horbulin has foreign awards. He is the honoured mechanical engineer of Ukraine (1994) and was given the Certificate of Honour of Verkhovna Rada of Ukraine (January 2004).

V. Horbulin's studies have touched upon problems of system analysis and theory of designing complex technical systems and development of the systematic and conceptual framework of Ukraine's national security strategy.

Volodymyr Horbulin made a significant contribution to the establishment of scientific and methodological fundamentals of the national security system, development of the defence component within the military-and-strategic and military-and-technical policy, reformation of the defence and industrial complex and the security sector.

Oleksandr Belov

Born on 3 February 1951 in Zaporizhzhia, Ukraine, O. Belov is an adviser to the head of the Security Service of Ukraine. He is married and has a son.

Mr. Belov is author and co-author of over 43 publications.

He played a crucial role in the Security Service reform process. He has worked on bringing the security sector of Ukraine closer to European and Euro-Atlantic standards.

Mr. Belov graduated from the Zaporizhzhia Technical School for Electronic Devices, Department of History, Zaporizhzhia State Pedagogical Institute. He received the Honoured Scientist and Technician of Ukraine (2001) award.

Since 1979, Mr. Belov has worked at the State Security Institutions. From 1994 to 1996 he was head of the Information and Analytical Directorate of the Security Service of Ukraine.

In 1996 he became deputy head of the Security Service of Ukraine.

From 1999 to 2001 he was acting director of the National Institute for Strategic Studies under the National Security and Defence Council of Ukraine, and deputy secretary of the National Security and Defence Council of Ukraine.

In 2001 he was deputy head of the Presidential Administration and after October 2001 adviser to the head of the Security Service of Ukraine.

From 2000 to 2001 he was head of the Ukrainian part of the sub-commission on the issues of the functioning of the Russian Black Sea Fleet in Ukraine of the Ukrainian-Russian Cooperation Commission. During this time, he was appointed head of the Ukrainian part of the High-level Joint Working Group on Defence Reform.

From 2003 to 2005 he acted as head of the Working Group of the State Commission on Reformation and Development of the Armed Forces of Ukraine.

He was co-chair of the Ukraine-NATO Working Group on Democratic and Civil Control of the Intelligence Sector from 2006 to 2008 and since 2008 he has been the Ukrainian co-chair of the NATO-Ukraine Staff Talks on Intelligence Sector Reform in Ukraine.

Oleksandr V. Lytvynenko

O. Lytvynenko—doctor of political science, senior research associate, colonel in reserve, author of over 100 scientific papers and publications, including three sole monographs—was born on 27 April 1972 in Kyiv city.

In July 1994, O. Lytvynenko received a mathematician's diploma (applied mathematics) at the Institute of Cryptography and Informatics of Russian Fss Academy, Moscow city. In March 1998, after having defended his thesis on political problems of intentional systems and global development, Mr. Lytvynenko obtained a Ph.D. in political science, which he defended at the National Institute for Strategic Studies in October 2002. In April 2003, he became a senior research associate for fundamentals of the state national security. In March 2009, O. Lytvynenko got the Specialist's Diploma in Legal Science, National Taras Shevchenko University of Kyiv.

From September 1997 to July 2007, Oleksandr Lytvynenko worked as an assistant lecturer at the Institute of International Relations, National Taras Shevchenko University of Kyiv. From August 1994 to August 1998, he was an officer, chief officer, and chief specialist of the Department of Information Protection under the Main Department of State Communications at the Security Service of Ukraine. From August 1998 to May 2007, O. Lytvynenko worked as a senior consultant, head of the department, deputy director and first deputy director of the National Institute for Strategic Studies. In May 2005, he took the post of head of the Department of State Security, head of the Expert Commission, and head of the Department of State Security Issues under the National Security and Defence Council of Ukraine. In December 2007, he became the deputy head of the Department on Information and Analytical Support at the Security Service of Ukraine. Since August 2009, he has worked as the adviser to the director of the Institute of National Security Problems at the National Security and Defence Council of Ukraine.

From April to May 2002, Oleksandr Lytvynenko attended a course on analytics in international relations at York University in Toronto, Canada.

From April to May 2005, he was trained on national security issues at the Marshall Center, Garmisch-Partenkirchen, Germany.

Geneva Centre for the Democratic Control of Armed Forces (DCAF)

Timothy Donais (Ed.)
Local Ownership and Security Sector Reform
The notion of "local ownership" has emerged in recent years as part of the contemporary commonsense of security sector reform (SSR). While the argument that externally driven reform processes are unsustainable is now widely accepted, the principle of local ownership has proven difficult to both define and operationalise. With contributions by leading practitioners, both "insiders" and "outsiders", *Local Ownership and Security Sector Reform* subjects the broader issue of local ownership to critical scrutiny, furthers the debate on what local ownership is and why it matters, and explores how ownership issues have played out in the context of specific SSR case studies.
2008, 312 S., 29,90 €, br., ISBN 978-3-8258-1652-0